CONTENTS

Student Leadership Practices Inventory

FACILITATOR'S GUIDE
SECOND EDITION

James M. Kouzes

Barry Z. Posner, Ph.D.

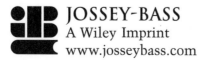

JOSSEY-BASS
A Wiley Imprint
www.josseybass.com

ISBN: 0-7879-8029-3

Published by Jossey-Bass
A Wiley Imprint
989 Market Street, San Francisco, CA 94103-1741   www.josseybass.com

The materials that appear in this book (except those for which reprint permission must be obtained from the primary sources) may be reproduced for educational/training activities. We do, however, require that the following statement appear on all reproductions:

Student Leadership Practices Inventory by James M. Kouzes and Barry Z. Posner.
Copyright © 2006 by James M. Kouzes and Barry Z. Posner.

This free permission is limited to the reproduction of material for educational/training events. Systematic or large-scale reproduction or distribution (more than one hundred copies per year)—or inclusion of items in publications for sale—may be done only with prior written permission. Also, reproduction on computer disk or by any other electronic means requires prior written permission. Requests to the Publisher for permission should be addressed to the Permissions Department, John Wiley & Sons, Inc., 111 River Street, Hoboken, NJ 07030, 201-748-6011, fax 201-748-6008, or online at http://www.wiley.com/go/permissions.

Readers should be aware that Internet websites offered as citations and/or sources for further information may have changed or disappeared between the time this was written and when it is read.

Jossey-Bass books and products are available through most bookstores. To contact Jossey-Bass directly call our Customer Care Department within the U.S. at 800-956-7739, outside the U.S. at 317-572-3986, or fax 317-572-4002.

Jossey-Bass also publishes its books in a variety of electronic formats. Some content that appears in print may not be available in electronic books.

Printed in the United States of America

SECOND EDITION

PB Printing 10 9 8 7 6 5 4 3 2 1

1 Introduction

Leadership is everyone's business. Our research has shown that leadership is an observable, learnable set of practices. It is not something mystical and ethereal that cannot be understood by ordinary people. We believe that, given the opportunity for feedback and practice, those with the desire and persistence to lead can substantially improve their abilities to do so.

Many young people taking a leadership course for the first time already have more leadership experience than they realize. For example, they may have trained and supervised peers in an employment setting or volunteer activity, started a club, or captained a sports team. A leadership development survey is not only a means of learning leadership skills but also a way of discovering or examining the leadership experiences students may have had already.

The purpose of this *Facilitator's Guide* is to assist you in designing and conducting a leadership program based on the *Student Leadership Practices Inventory (Student LPI)*. Using this manual in conjunction with the *Student LPI,* you will be able to accomplish the following:

- Present a valid, understandable, and practical model of leadership for students.
- Provide reliable and useful feedback to students on their current use of a specific set of leadership behaviors.
- Conduct a workshop (from one hour to a half-day or full day) on leadership.
- Integrate the *Student LPI* into other leadership development programs.

The *Leadership Practices Inventory* was created as part of an extensive and continuing research project into the everyday actions and behaviors of exemplary leaders—at all levels, across a variety of organizational settings. Our book, *The Leadership Challenge,* provides a comprehensive explanation of the empirical and conceptual basis for the practices and behaviors that are the foundation of this instrument*. The book offers numerous suggestions for improving skills in these practices and behaviors. Consequently, we strongly recommend that all facilitators read this book prior to conducting a workshop or program in which the *Student LPI* will be used. Students also benefit from reading the book, often as a follow-up to their workshop or classroom participation. Also available for students is *The Five Practices of Exemplary Student Leadership* article.

We wish you every success in your efforts to liberate the leader within each student.

James M. Kouzes   Barry Z. Posner, Ph.D.
Orinda, California   *Santa Clara, California*

The Student LPI Components

Component	What It Is	Purpose
SLPI-Self	Student leader version of the thirty-item questionnaire for self-assessment of frequency of use of The Five Practices	Used by student leaders to rate themselves on the thirty leadership behaviors
SLPI-Observer	Observer version of the thirty-item questionnaire asking for constituent's assessment of a student leader's frequency of use of The Five Practices	Used by observers to rate student leaders on the thirty leadership behaviors
SLPI Scoring Software CD-ROM	Software program that enables facilitator or administrator to enter data from the *Student LPI* questionnaires and generate individual and group reports; also includes Power-Point versions of visuals from Appendix B and Appendix E of the *Facilitator's Guide*	Makes it easy to enter, retrieve, and store individual *Student LPI* data and reports and to track improvement over time. Provides masters of the visuals essential to the presentation of The Five Practices model and to guiding students through analysis and interpretation of *SLPI* data

---

* To purchase this book or for further information, contact Jossey-Bass, 989 Market Street, San Francisco, CA 94103; phone: (800) 274–4434. Or look on our website: www.theleadershipchallenge.com. *The Jossey-Bass Academic Administrator's Guide to Exemplary Leadership* provides an application of this framework to a higher education setting, useful for both staff and faculty leadership development.

Component	What It Is	Purpose
SLPI Feedback Report	The document produced by the *SLPI* Scoring Software that summarizes the data from Self and Observer questionnaires by practice, behaviors, and percentile ranking; also generates optional group and multiple administration reports	Provides student leaders with valid, reliable feedback on their leadership behaviors
SLPI Facilitator's Guide	A comprehensive guide that includes information about the development of the *SLPI*, descriptions of The Five Practices, an explanation of the *SLPI* Feedback Report, instructor scripts, and more	Provides detailed information to help facilitator design and conduct *SLPI* workshop
SLPI Student Workbook	A step-by-step workbook for students' use in *SLPI* workshop	Provides instructions, information, questions, and worksheets students use during a workshop to record their observation and interpretations while they analyze their Feedback Reports and to develop personal action plans following an initial feedback session
Student Leadership Planner	A comprehensive workbook that includes tips on best learning practices, developmental ideas for each of The Five Practices, along with progress recording and follow-up action planning guides	Provides a tool that student leaders can use after the *Student LPI* workshop to continue their learning and development on an ongoing basis
The Five Practices article	A monograph that presents a concise overview of The Five Practices, case examples, and overall thoughts on leadership	

2

Origin of the
Student Leadership
Practices Inventory

Most of the leadership development programs designed for college students are based on studies and models that were developed for managers in business and public-sector organizations.[1] Serious questions can be raised about whether such models and their concomitant instruments are applicable to college students and collegiate environments, which differ considerably from the environments in which managers operate. One substantive literature review concluded that "valid instruments designed specifically for college students to measure their leadership development did not exist."[2] This assertion is still true today. The *Student Leadership Practices Inventory (SLPI)* was developed to fill this gap.

The *Student LPI* has two forms: Self and Observer. Each form consists of thirty statements—six statements to measure each of The Five Practices of Exemplary Student Leadership®. The forms differ only in the individuals who complete them. The *Student LPI-Self* form is completed by the student leader himself or herself, and the *Student LPI-Observer* form is completed by a person who has directly observed the leadership behaviors of that student leader. During the workshop or course, students compare the two sets of responses to discover their strengths or areas for improvement as leaders. Within the course or workshop, facilitators can take students through a series of exercises to help them better understand and develop The Five Practices.

Instrument Development

In developing the original *Leadership Practices Inventory (LPI)*, case studies from over 2,500 managers about their personal-best experiences as leaders were collected. Content analyses of these case studies suggested a pattern of behaviors and actions used by people when they were most effective as leaders: Model the Way, Inspire a Shared Vision, Challenge the Process, Enable Others to Act, and Encourage the Heart.[3] The development of a student version of the instrument followed the same case-study approach to investigate whether the leadership behaviors of college students were comparable with those of managers.[4]

The initial student group consisted of outstanding student leaders at a large urban state university campus, as demonstrated by their nomination for a nationally prominent leadership development experience for college students. Four students were randomly selected by year in school (junior or senior) and gender (male or female) to participate in this stage of the research project. The students were asked to think about their personal-best leadership experiences and to make notes about the behaviors they believed were most critical to the success of their endeavors.

One week later, in a structured-interview format, each student responded to specific questions based on the personal-best survey reported in *The Leadership Challenge*. The interviews lasted between thirty and ninety minutes; each was tape-recorded with the respondent's consent. The student interviews were content-analyzed for themes (sentences or phrases) about leadership actions and behaviors. These themes were coded and tabulated into the five leadership categories that had been originally proposed from private-sector and public-sector managers. These findings indicated that college student leaders did engage in these leadership practices and that this conceptual framework was relevant to the college student's leadership experience. A recent study followed a similar process for validating the appropriateness of the personal-best leadership case study methodology and *Student LPI* for use with college students.[5]

Pilot-Testing the *Student LPI*

Each statement on the original *LPI* was assessed in terms of its congruence with the themes derived from case studies of students' personal-best leadership experiences. The purpose of this coding was to determine which *LPI* statements accurately reflected the behavior of *student* leaders, thus facilitating the process of identifying terminology and concepts appropriate for use with a college-student population. Using this data, items were modified as necessary for use in the pilot version of the *Student LPI*.

The pilot version of the *Student LPI* consisted of thirty descriptive statements paralleling those found in the original *LPI*. Each of the five leadership practices was assessed with six statements on the *Student LPI*, and each was measured with a five-point Likert scale (where 1 meant "rarely" and 5 meant "very frequently"). The statements focused on leadership *behaviors* and on the *frequency* with which the individual engaged in those particular behaviors.

Twenty-three members from the student senate at a small private suburban college campus were asked to serve as the test site for studying the pilot version of the *Student LPI*. After these students completed the pilot version, they participated in an item-by-item discussion to determine whether any test statements were ambiguous, confusing, or not applicable to their experience as student leaders. This discussion was tape-recorded. Of the thirty test items, twenty-five (83 percent) were unanimously determined to be clear and understandable and to consist of terminology and concepts that were within students' and student leaders' experience. Ways to improve the somewhat problematic remaining items were also discussed and determined. Five student leaders who had not been involved with any of the earlier *Student LPI* efforts were invited to participate in a focus-group discussion of the revised *Student LPI,* and only very minor editorial changes were suggested.

Empirical Studies

A large number of empirical studies using the *Student LPI* have been conducted.[6] For example, fraternity chapter presidents across the United States completed the *Student LPI-Self* and had the members of their executive committees complete the *Student LPI-Observer.* The members of the executive committees also assessed the effectiveness of their chapter presidents along several dimensions, for example: building team spirit, representing the chapter to administrators and alumni, meeting chapter objectives, facilitating volunteers, and so on. The most effective chapter presidents engaged in each of the five leadership practices significantly more frequently than did their less effective counterparts. Multiple-regression analyses showed that these leadership practices accounted for 65 percent of the variance in assessments of chapter presidents' effectiveness.[7]

A study of sorority chapter presidents from across the United States paralleled the previous study both in design and in findings. The most effective sorority chapter presidents engaged in each of the five leadership practices significantly more frequently than did their less effective counterparts. These leadership practices accounted for 80 percent of the variance in assessments of chapter presidents' effectiveness in multiple-regression analyses.[8] Together, these two studies also demonstrated that the practices of effective student leaders did not vary according to the leader's gender. Effective chapter presidents, whether male or female, engaged in the five leadership practices significantly more than did the less effective student leaders. This was true from both the leaders' own perspective and from the perspective of people in their organizations.[9] Few gender differences among college students have been reported, from populations ranging from Greek chapter leaders in the Midwest[10] to first-year undergraduates[11] to students enrolled in either hospitality management or dietetics programs.[12]

Sample populations of resident advisors (RAs) from seven diverse collegiate environments were studied.[13] Not only did RAs complete the *Student LPI-Self* and distribute *Student LPI-Observers* to residents in their housing facility, but effectiveness data across several different sources—the RAs, the students living in their residential units, and the resident director of each campus—were collected and a remarkably consistent pattern was found. Those who engaged in the five leadership practices most frequently, as compared to those who engaged in them less often, viewed themselves as more effective and were also viewed as more effective by their supervisors and by their constituents. No significant interaction effects between gender and performance were found. This finding is consistent with other studies involving RAs and their residents.[14]

The impact of leadership behaviors was also investigated for students serving as orientation advisors.[15] In this study, incoming college students completed both the *Student LPI-Observer* and an evaluation of their orientation advisors' effectiveness. Although together for just a few days, and in an arbitrary relationship in the sense that the members of the groups neither selected one another nor selected (or elected) their leader (the orientation advisor), the effectiveness of orientation advisors, consistent with previous studies, was directly related to the extent to which they engaged in the five key leadership practices. Self-reports by the orientation advisors showed a strong positive relationship between perceptions of effectiveness and the frequency that they reported engaging in these leadership practices.

How leadership practices might be affected by various characteristics of the group or setting that students are involved with has been the focus of additional studies.[16] For instance, students who were compensated for being leaders did not systematically engage in a different pattern of leadership practices when compared with those who were uncompensated for their leadership responsibilities. Student leaders working with peers in a nonhierarchical relationship did not engage in these leadership practices more or less significantly than those students who were elected by their peers into official positions of leadership or who held a hierarchical position in a student organization (such as president). Others have reported that the leadership practices were not related to a student's gender, race, age, work outside the home, full- or part-time student status, or semester in school.[17]

In addition, it has been demonstrated that students do not vary their leadership practices when involved in a one-time leadership project versus a project or program lasting for an entire academic year.[18] However, students who returned for a second year in a leadership position or had taken a leadership course generally engaged in each of the five leadership practices more often than their counterparts.[19] Several studies have shown that participation in a leadership development program resulted in significantly higher leadership practices scores compared to those students who had not been through a program. These findings were independent of such demographic variables as year in school, family cluster affiliation, gender, GPA, Greek affiliation, or ethnicity.[20]

While the previous discussion generally focused on validity, as a psychometric instrument the *Student LPI* has generally shown strong reliability. Early studies reported internal reliability scores (Cronbach alpha) of $\alpha = .68$ for Model, $\alpha = .79$ for Inspire, $\alpha = .66$ for Challenge, $\alpha = .70$ for Enable, and $\alpha = .80$ for Encourage, and these are relatively consistent with more recent findings.[21] In addition, test-retest reliability of the *Student LPI,* over a ten-week period, has been demonstrated as statistically significant, with correlations exceeding $r = .51$.[22] Tests of social desirability bias have not shown statistically significant relationships with *Student LPI* scores.[23]

Overall, the *Student LPI* shows consistent relationships with various measures of effectiveness, as reported across multiple constituencies. Moreover, the *Student LPI* is robust across different collegiate student populations (for example, fraternities, sororities, residence halls, orientation programs, academic majors, and the like). It is relatively independent of various demographic variables (gender, age, ethnicity, and so on) but possibly affected by previous leadership experiences and leadership course work.

Notes

1. F. H. Freeman, K. B. Knott, and M. K. Schwartz, *Leadership Education 1994–1995: A Sourcebook*. Greensboro, NC: Center for Creative Leadership, 1994.
2. B. Brodsky, "Development of a Modified Version of the *Leadership Practices Inventory* for Use with College Students," unpublished master's thesis, San Jose State University, 1988.
3. The conceptual origin of the original *Leadership Practices Inventory* is best described in *The Leadership Challenge*. Information about the empirical development and psychometric properties of the *LPI* can be found in: J. M. Kouzes and B. Z. Posner, "Development and Validation of the *Leadership Practices Inventory*," *Educational and Psychological Measurement*, 1988, *48*(2):483–496; J. M. Kouzes and B. Z. Posner, "Leadership Practices: An Alternative to the Psychological Perspective," in K. Clark and M. Clark (Eds.) *Measures of Leadership* (West Orange, NJ: Leadership Library of America, 1990); and J. M. Kouzes and B. Z. Posner, "Psychometric Properties of the Leadership Practices Inventory – Updated," *Educational and Psychological Measurement*, 1993, *53*(1):191–199.
4. More complete information about this initial research project is available in Brodsky, 1988 (see note 2). See also B. Z. Posner and B. Brodsky, "A Leadership Development Instrument for College Students," *Journal of College Student Development*, 1992, *33*(4):231–237.
5. S. Arendt, "Leadership Behaviors in Undergraduate Hospitality Management and Dietetics Students," unpublished doctoral dissertation, Iowa State University, 2004.
6. For a recent review of the literature, see B. Z. Posner, "A Leadership Development Instrument for Students: Updated," *Journal of College Student Development*, 2004, *45*(4):443–456.
7. Posner and Brodsky, 1992 (see note 4).
8. B. Z. Posner and B. Brodsky, "Leadership Practices of Effective Student Leaders: Gender Makes No Difference," *NASPA Journal*, 1994, *31*(2):113–120; and B. Z. Posner, 2004 (see note 6).
9. Posner and Brodsky, 1994.
10. T. Adams and M. Keim, "Leadership Practices and Effectiveness Among Greek Student Leaders," *College Student Journal*, 2002, *34*:259–270.
11. M. Mendez-Grant, "A Study of Freshman Interest Groups and Leadership Practices at Texas Women's University," unpublished doctoral dissertation, University of North Texas, 2001.
12. Arendt, 2004 (see note 5).
13. B. Z. Posner and B. Brodsky, "The Leadership Practices of Effective RAs," *Journal of College Student Development*, 1993, *34*(4):300–304.
14. M. Levy, "Followers' Perceptions of Leaders: Prototypes and Perceptions of Resident Assistants," unpublished masters' thesis, University of Maryland, 1995.
15. B. Z. Posner and J. Rosenberger, "Effective Orientation Advisors Are Leaders Too," *NASPA Journal*, 1997, *35*(1):46–56.
16. B. Z. Posner and J. Rosenberger, "The Impact of Situational Factors on Students' Leadership Behaviors," working paper, Leavey School of Business, Santa Clara University, 1998.
17. L. M. Edington, "College Classroom Leadership Practices: What Gender Has to Do with It," unpublished doctoral dissertation, Ball State University, 1995.
18. Posner and Rosenberger, 1998 (see note 16).
19. For example: Arendt, 2004 (note 5); W. Baxter, "Engineering Leadership," unpublished master's thesis, Texas A&M University, 2001; Levy, 1995 (note 14); and Posner and Rosenberger, 1998 (note 16).
20. For example: Mendez-Grant, 2001 (note 11); and D. Pugh, "College Student Leadership Development: Program Impact on Student Participation," unpublished doctoral dissertation, University of Georgia, 2001.
21. Posner, 2004 (see note 6).
22. Pugh, 2001 (see note 20).
23. J. Walker, "Leadership Development of Students Engaged in Experiential Learning: Implications for Internship Programs in Textiles and Apparel," unpublished doctoral dissertation, University of North Carolina at Greensboro, 2001.

3

The Five Practices of Exemplary Student Leadership®

In this section we summarize the five practices of exemplary leaders and associated behaviors that form the foundation of the *Student LPI*. (More in-depth descriptions of each leadership practice can be found in *The Leadership Challenge*.) At the end of each summary are two behavioral commitments that leaders make to put the practice into use (see also Visuals 2A and 2B, "The Ten Commitments of Leadership," in Appendix B). Students and young adults may find they have already demonstrated these practices and commitments in many of their activities—for instance, on sports teams, in school or on campus, in church groups, or in clubs and other organizations. The *Student LPI* will enable many to consider the leadership skills they already possess as well as to explore the skills they want to develop.

Model the Way

Leaders have a philosophy—a set of high standards by which the organization is measured, a set of values about how others in the organization should be treated, and a set of principles that make the organization unique and distinctive. Leaders stand up for their beliefs and show by their own example how others ought to behave. Leaders build their credibility by maintaining consistency between their words and deeds.

Being a role model requires clarity about personal values. Focusing other people's energies and commitments requires developing an alignment between the values of the leader and others in the organization.

The commitments of leaders to *Model the Way* involve

- **Finding your voice** by clarifying your personal values
- **Setting the example** by aligning actions with shared values

Note: The following case studies also appear in Chapter One of the *Student Workbook*.

While Jason Hegland was the captain of his water polo team, he learned the hard way about how to be the team leader: "First, I was just plain bossy. I was also stubborn. Things were supposed to go *my* way. Worst of all, I didn't show anyone else what they meant to the team as a whole. I cut people down when I should have built them up." Luckily, early in the season, a teammate brought these flaws to his attention, and, to his credit, Jason reflected on what was really important and quickly made changes, in his words, "to show everyone how a real captain acts."

One of the first things he did was to get himself to school every day at 5:00 A.M. for practice. When he saw other players during the day, he would ask them why they weren't at practice. Soon enough, Jason said, "The message about practices sunk in and we had 100 percent attendance." He also opened up communications. Every day he asked his teammates: "What didn't we do well yesterday that we need to work on today?" He asked those who were better players than he was what he needed to do to improve himself. Furthermore, Jason stopped focusing on errors and became the "head cheerleader" for the team, mentioning at each postgame meeting at least one good thing that each of his teammates had done.

As for results, Jason pointed out that, while the changes he made in his leadership style didn't lead his team to the state championship, it was the first time that any school from a Chicago suburb placed within the top ten, and most importantly, he said, "That year the team members were the closest that they had ever been to one another." The lesson for Jason: "I learned that those who follow you are only as good as the model you present them with."

Inspire a Shared Vision

There is no freeway to the future; often there are not even paved roads, only uncertain terrain and wilderness, so pioneering leaders rely on a compass and a dream. They look to the future with a sense of what is uniquely possible and passionately believe that people working together can make a difference. Vision is the leader's magnetic north; it gives direction and purpose to the organization.

A leader's vision is insufficient to create organized movement. Leaders must enlist others in a common vision by appealing to their values, interests, hopes, and dreams so that others clearly understand and accept the vision as their own.

Leaders breathe life into their vision with strong appeals and quiet persuasion, generating enthusiasm and excitement for the common vision. They see a future full of possibilities.

The commitments of leaders to *Inspire a Shared Vision* involve

- **Envisioning the future** by imagining exciting and ennobling possibilities
- **Enlisting others** in a common vision by appealing to shared aspirations

The insight for Filip Morovich was learning that "leadership is not about being the great heroic solver of all problems; it is about inspiring people to believe that the problem can be solved by working together." In one of Filip's classes, the assignment was to produce a one-hour musical play (with singing, dancing, and all the rest!) on some historical theme. Pretty much everyone in the class was afraid and daunted by this task because few of them had any theater experience or particular acting talents. Filip described the scene: "The group was adrift and everyone was sitting around staring at one another in stark silence. I got very angry inside, and at that instant I had a vision. A real flash of lightning in my mind made it clear to me that we could be successful. But at this point it was only my idea, only my flash of inspiration, and so I had to share it and make it a common belief among us all."

He decided some drama was necessary to get everyone's attention, so he picked up his pen, raised it high in the air, and dropped it onto the binder on his lap. A bomb going off in the room could not have been louder. This had the intended effect and Filip launched into inspiring a shared vision: "I used a hopeful and positive tone of voice. I was excited and called on our collective strength as a team to move forward and be successful. I hoped that my excitement and positive mood would prove infectious and revitalize the group. We all noticed an uplift of our mood and we could literally see a sparkle of hope returning to one another's eyes. The key was making the vision of our success a joint process because we all came to believe that we could do this."

Challenge the Process

Challenge is the opportunity for greatness. Maintaining the status quo breeds mediocrity. Leaders seek and accept challenging opportunities to test their abilities and look for innovative ways to improve the organization. People do their best when there is a chance to change the way things are. Leaders motivate others to exceed their limits.

Most innovations, however, do not spring directly from the leader. Leaders realize that good ideas come through the ears—not the mouth—and listen to the counsel of the people who use their services and products and the people who do the work.

Leadership is closely associated with change and innovation; the quest for change is an adventure and the training ground for leaders. For leaders to get the best from themselves and others, they must find the task enjoyable and intrinsically rewarding. Leaders are experimenters. They find ways to get outside the imaginary boundaries of organizational convention. They take risks—and focus on mistakes as learning opportunities.

Leaders get people started by convincing them that the impossible is possible and by taking the first step themselves. Breaking problems into manageable pieces keeps people from being overwhelmed. Planning small victories makes the larger goal seem achievable. Small wins breed success and set the stage for building commitment to the new path.

The commitments of leaders to *Challenge the Process* involve

- **Searching for opportunities** by seeking innovative ways to change, grow, and improve
- **Experimenting and taking risks** by constantly generating small wins and learning from mistakes

Allison Avon told us that the idea of Challenging the Process took on real meaning for her when she was in charge of her school's annual Charity Fashion Show. The school typically raised funds to buy toys for the children at a local Head Start program. For various reasons the program administrators didn't want the school to buy the children toys, and "we couldn't convince them otherwise." Everyone was pretty discouraged and wanted to cancel the fashion show.

Allison wasn't ready to give up, so she asked everyone for their ideas and what alternatives they could imagine. As a result they decided, "Perhaps if we bought the children educational items such as books instead of toys, then maybe the Head Start program administrators would be more receptive." In the end the fashion show and their day with the children—sharing and reading books together—were great successes. As Allison reported: "The results were better than we could have hoped for. This process of trial and error gave me a new perspective on what is required of a successful leader. When the process challenges you," Allison retorts, "challenge back."

Enable Others to Act

Leaders know that they cannot do it alone. It takes partners to get extraordinary things done in an organization. Leaders create an atmosphere of mutual trust and respect. They build teams that feel like a family and make people feel like owners, not like hired hands.

Getting people to work together begins with creating cooperative goals and sustaining trusting relationships. Leaders understand how being trustworthy is the reciprocal of trusting others. They make sure that when they win, everyone wins.

Empowering others is essentially the process of turning followers into leaders themselves. Leaders realize how power is not a fixed-sum quantity but an expandable resource. The process of strengthening others is facilitated when people work on tasks that are critical to the organization's success, when they exercise discretion and autonomy in their efforts, when their accomplishments are visible and recognized by others, and when they are well connected to other people of influence and support.

The commitments leaders make to *Enable Others to Act* involve

- **Fostering collaboration** by promoting cooperative goals and building trust
- **Strengthening others** by sharing power and discretion

With beads of sweat dripping down his face, Peter Freeman continued to attack the nails with his hammer. It was a blazing hot day in Harlan, Kentucky, and he and his classmates had to finish the roof by the end of the week; but it was already Thursday and the roof was not close to being finished. "As I looked around," said Peter, "I saw a group of kids who were unmotivated, tired, and hot." He began nailing again, thinking to himself, "We have got to finish this roof." He looked up again and saw another possibility: a group of highly motivated, energetic people who would work together to accomplish the task. It began to dawn on Peter that "merely working hard on my own would not allow us to reach the goal of finishing the roof in another day."

So he set out to enable those around him, reminding them of the purpose and urgency of their task and how important it was for them to work together as a team. "This brought about an amazing change," he reported, and "rejuvenated and reenergized, my friends attacked their work with vigor." Peter realized that he could not accomplish "my goals on my own without the help of a team." The key was to involve others in making key decisions and sharing ideas about how to best accomplish "OUR" goal. "I asked for their opinions," Peter explained, "finding out from them what they thought was the best way to go about things." In fact, before he realized it, others got excited and took on new responsibilities, making choices and acting like leaders themselves . . . and the job was done!

Encourage the Heart

Getting extraordinary things done in organizations is hard work. The climb to the summit is arduous and steep. Leaders encourage others to continue the quest. They give heart by visibly recognizing people's contributions to the common vision. They express pride in the accomplishments of their teams. They make people feel like heroes by telling the rest of the organization about what these individuals and the team have accomplished.

Leaders have high expectations both of themselves and of their constituents. They provide people with clear direction, substantial encouragement, personal attention, and meaningful feedback. Leaders make people feel like winners, and winning people like to continue raising the stakes!

Celebrating team accomplishments adds fun to hard work and reinforces team spirit. Celebrations increase people's network of connections and promote information sharing. Fostering high-quality interpersonal relationships enhances productivity along with both physical and psychological health.

The commitments of leaders to *Encourage the Heart* involve

- **Recognizing contributions** by showing appreciation for individual excellence
- **Celebrating the values and victories** by creating a spirit of community

"Being a leader on my volleyball team," Kirsten Cornell explained, "forced me to learn lessons about encouragement and put them into practice." One of her main goals was to create a positive atmosphere on the team: "So I made sure that I recognized people for making good plays with gestures as simple as high-fives and words of praise (and my teammates got in the habit of doing the same)." As Kirsten put it: "I found that encouraging my teammates was one of the easiest and most beneficial thing I could do to make the team better."

Kirsten said that part of creating an uplifting attitude on the team was letting the players know that she had confidence in them: "I showed my teammates with both words and actions that I believed in them. With words I would tell them that I knew they could make a perfect pass or get a great hit. With actions I showed them my belief in them in a tangible way by spreading out the sets between players so that everyone had a chance to get into the game." Also critical, she said, was "taking an honest interest in each player. I got to know my teammates as both people and athletes. I knew the things they were dealing with outside of the thirty-foot square where we met to play, and this allowed me to realize when they needed extra encouragement and support."

Finally, Kirsten created a culture of celebration by acknowledging accomplishments, however small they might have been, both on and off the court (for example, having birthday cards signed by everyone on the team). "This culture," she explained, "caused us to have fun while we worked and to take pride in what we achieved together."

4

Preparing for the *Student LPI* Feedback Workshop

In this workshop students receive feedback from the results of their *Student LPI,* then assess their strengths and note areas for improvement in their leadership skills. For those using the *Student LPI* as part of a course (as opposed to a workshop), this design can easily be adapted to a classroom situation within a single or multiple class session, seminar, or course framework.

Objectives

As a result of this session, students will be better able to

- Understand the specific behaviors and actions of exemplary leadership.
- Identify their personal strengths as leaders.
- Identify areas for improving their leadership practices.
- Determine actions for becoming better leaders by increasing the frequency and comfort (skill) with which they engage in various leadership behaviors.
- Plan how to share their results and learning from the *Student LPI* feedback session with others in their organization.

Physical Setting

Students begin at round tables in the main seminar room for an overview lecture on the *Student LPI* and interpretation of their results. Following some individual reflection, they may cluster together in groups of two or three people for further discussion among themselves but should be together again in the main seminar room for closing comments on this session.

Materials

- Erasable whiteboard or newsprint flip chart
- Computer projector and screen (for PowerPoint presentation) or overhead projector and screen for transparencies*
- Copies of *Student LPI-Self* forms (if inventory is to be administered during workshop or class)
- Copies of *Student LPI-Observer* forms
- Copies of *Student LPI Student Workbook*
- *Student LPI* Feedback Reports for *each* participant

Optional Materials

- Student Leadership Planner
- The Five Practices of Exemplary Student Leadership® article

Group Size

Workshops using the *Student LPI* can be conducted with groups as small as four and as large as several hundred people. A group of twenty to thirty-two people is optimal, especially if only one facilitator is involved. One of the important parts of the workshop is the opportunity for students to obtain assistance from the facilitator in interpreting the *Student LPI* Feedback Report. This should be considered when determining the size of the group and length of the workshop. The workshop includes activities for individuals, dyads or triads, and the total group.

Time Requirements

The workshop described in this manual can be conducted within as short a session as one hour or as long as four hours or even a full day, as well as across one or more class sessions. The time required varies depending on whether the session is one-time or part of a longer workshop on leadership or other management development issues. The time varies as well, depending on whether feedback from only the *Student LPI-Self* is provided or *Student LPI-Observer* data is also available, and according to how much introspection and action planning by students is desired.

Pre-Session Activities

The workshop may be designed to include completion of the *Student LPI-Self* within the workshop session itself or the *Student LPI-Self* may be completed

---

*PowerPoint files are provided on the *Student Leadership Practices Inventory* Scoring Software CD-ROM. See Appendix B for visuals for duplication onto transparencies.

by participants prior to the workshop. If the instrument is to be administered during the workshop, a copy of the *Student LPI-Self* should be distributed to each student. The *Student LPI Student Workbook* contains the scoring instructions and observer evaluation information that will be distributed and used later in the workshop.

The *Student LPI-Self* and *Observer* each take about eight to ten minutes to complete. Manually recording and scoring one *Student LPI-Self* and five *Student LPI-Observers* takes about fifteen minutes.

The preferred option is to have students complete the *Student LPI-Self* and *Observer* prior to attending the workshop. This heightens their interest in the workshop, where they can receive their "scores" and find out how they are doing. The motivation level is heightened when students know they will also be receiving feedback from other people (via the *Student LPI-Observer*) at the workshop. *Student LPI* data can also be collected as a pre- and post-test assessment in situations in which that is appropriate.

If a primary goal of the workshop is to help students assess their own strengths and areas for improvement as leaders, then we strongly recommend that students have the *Student LPI-Observer* completed by other people who interact and work with them. The combination of self-perceptions and others' perceptions greatly enhances the value of the feedback.

If they are using *Student LPI-Observer* forms, students should be instructed, at the time they receive their *Student LPI-Self* as pre-work, to distribute a *Student LPI-Observer* to each individual from whom they would like to receive feedback regarding their leadership behavior. It is preferable to solicit completion of at least five to eight *Student LPI-Observers* (which allows for one or two people to not return or complete them, for whatever reason), but more observers can be invited to participate. It is not necessary to have everyone in the student leader's organization complete the *Student LPI-Observer* (using the principle of "sampling" a population from statistical theory).

Participants put their names on their own *Student LPI-Self* and each copy of the *Student LPI-Observer* form *before* distribution. Both the *Student LPI-Self* and *Student LPI-Observer* are typically returned directly to the facilitator to make certain that feedback will be available at the workshop for participants. This also encourages confidentiality for those returning the *Student LPI-Observer.* We recommend that, when possible, *Student LPI* forms be returned at least one week prior to the start of the workshop or class session. This allows sufficient time for follow-up with those who have not returned their own forms or had their forms returned by others.

Important: On both the *Student LPI-Self* and the *Student LPI-Observer* forms, the information in the "Further Instructions" section on where the respondents are to return the forms should be filled out *before* distribution to students or observers, to avoid the forms being returned to the wrong place. Students can fill out the information for each of their *Student LPI-Observer* forms.

Note that the *Student LPI-Observer* forms are intended to be completed anonymously. This is also the preferred option when the *Leadership Practices Inventory* is used with managers and executives. Our studies have shown that people provide more reliable feedback when they don't have to reveal their identity to the leader (and this applies for both positive and negative reasons). The trade-off, however, is that sometimes the leader can't completely understand the feedback, especially individual responses that are at variance with everyone else's, without knowing the source. We suggest addressing this issue directly during the feedback session with student leaders.

5 Workshop Process Details

This chapter gives step-by-step instructions for conducting a workshop on The Five Practices of Exemplary Student Leadership®. The "you" in this section refers to the facilitator and generally assumes little or no prior experience with workshops such as this one. Times are approximate. Some optional steps are also included. Masters for creating overhead transparencies and handouts are provided in Appendix B. A PowerPoint presentation, which includes the visuals in Appendix B, is provided on the *Student LPI* Scoring Software CD-ROM.

Introduction   (5–10 MINUTES)

Begin with an overview of the session. If the students have completed the *Student LPI* prior to the session, tell them when they will receive their feedback shortly. If they will complete the *Student LPI* during the session, it should be completed either at this time or after you have led a discussion defining leadership.

Discussion on Leadership   (10–15 MINUTES)

Ask: "What Is Leadership?"

Seek several definitions and comments from the participants. Note their comments on a whiteboard or flip chart.

Lead a Discussion

Discuss how management and leadership are similar and how they are different. Write down salient points.

Write the Definition

After everyone has made a contribution, write the following definition of leadership on the whiteboard or flip chart. Explain that it will be used for the purposes of this workshop and that it was suggested by sociologist Vance Packard more than forty years ago in an influential book entitled *The Pyramid Climbers**:

> Leadership appears to be the art of getting others to want to do something you are convinced should be done.

Look at Key Words

Suggest to the group that the key words are "want to" and ask the students to discuss how the meaning differs when these two words are left out of the definition. (People often say it is then a definition of management.)

Discuss Internal Motivation

Explain that leadership is about internal motivation (getting others to "want to" do something). Talk some more about the concept.

Cover Other Phrases

Also direct everyone's attention to other critical phrases in the definition, such as "the art" (not the science), "getting others" (not doing it yourself), and "you are convinced" (leadership requires focus and commitment).

Write Another Definition

Next, write the following definition of leadership from *The Leadership Challenge* on the flip chart:

> The art of mobilizing others to want to struggle for shared aspirations.

Explain that of the more than two hundred definitions of leadership provided in the social science literature, all are generally compatible with the Kouzes and Posner leadership practices framework, which is the conceptual foundation for the *Student LPI.*

Warm-Up Activities   (OPTIONAL; 30–45 MINUTES)

Prepare students for a discussion of leadership by relating it to their own experiences in one of two ways: personal-best leadership experience and most admired leader.

---

*V. O. Packard, *The Pyramid Climbers.* New York: McGraw-Hill, 1962, p. 170.

Personal-Best Leadership Experience

Explain the Research. Explain that Kouzes and Posner researched leadership by seeking examples of the personal-best leadership experiences of more than 10,000 interviewees. Say that interviews were their primary means of collecting information about the times when people did their best as leaders. These case studies involved high school and college students, as well as people from around the globe, across a myriad of industries, disciplines, and backgrounds.

Ask for Their Own Experiences. Ask students to think about a time when they have been at their personal best as leaders and to identify five to seven key practices (strategies, behaviors, actions, and so on) that made a difference in that experience. Give them five to ten minutes for reflection and to make some notes for themselves. If you want, you can distribute a copy of Recalling a Personal-Best Leadership Experience (Appendix A), either within the workshop or as pre-work.

Form Small Groups. Put students into small groups. (The group size is dependent on how much time you want to allocate to this discussion. The time required increases with the number of people in the groups.) Ask them to describe their personal-best leadership experiences to one another and to explain the practices they used that made each such a good experience.

Find Common Themes. Ask the group members to listen for the common practices among the case studies presented in their small groups and to reach consensus about five to seven key practices that made the difference across all of their individual experiences. Have each group record their observations on newsprint sheets.

Have Groups Report Their Findings. Reassemble the total group. Have small groups report their observations about the most important practices, displaying their newsprint lists.

Look for Similarities. If time permits, after all the small groups have made their presentations, have the total group identify the practices that are similar across all the small groups.

Ask the students whether there was more similarity among their key leadership practices or differences across their leadership experiences. (The answer should overwhelmingly be "similarity.")

Most Admired Leader

An equally powerful but somewhat less personal way of engaging students in a discussion of leadership is to ask them to think about their most admired leader. This assignment could also be completed prior to the workshop.

Ask the Students for Their Most Admired Leaders. Start by asking:

Who is the person you most admire as a leader?

Encourage students to think of people they have had firsthand experience with, although some will undoubtedly select historical or contemporary public leaders.

Have Students Reflect. Have students reflect about and record their answers to the following questions:

What does (did) this person do?
What qualities does this person have that make you admire her or him as a leader?

Allow five to ten minutes for reflection and writing.

Form Small Groups. Form small groups in which each student relates to the other members the actions and qualities he or she has recorded. Tell everyone to listen for common elements and record their observations on newsprint.

Lead a Group Discussion. Bring the total group back together and have each small group give a brief report on its findings to the total group, displaying their newsprint lists. Tell the total group to look for common threads and generalizations that can be made. Discuss and list them for all to see.

Use what they have said to reinforce the notion that leadership is not something mysterious but comprises a learnable set of behaviors and skills. Note the commonalities in the behaviors and practices of those people we admire as leaders.

Completion of the *Student LPI-Self* (10 MINUTES)

If the instrument was completed before the session, skip this section.

Complete the Instrument

Following the instructions on the first page of the *Student LPI-Self,* ask students to complete pages 2 and 3 of their instruments, but not to score them yet.

Distribute the Student LPI-Observer

If students have not had others complete the *Student LPI-Observer* form prior to the workshop, give them copies now so that they can ask others to complete it later and then log the results on the scoring grids in the *Student Workbook.* It is also a good idea for them to ask other people to complete the *Student LPI-*

Observer in about three to six months, after they have had an opportunity to practice some of the behaviors they will learn in the workshop.

Lecture on The Five Practices of Exemplary Student Leadership® (20–40 MINUTES)

Before asking students to score the instrument, give a brief lecture on The Five Practices of Exemplary Student Leadership®, using visuals 1A through 1F and 2A through 2B in Appendix B and other material in this manual and in the *Student Leadership Practices Inventory Student Workbook*. You may also expand the lecture by using material from *The Leadership Challenge*.

Provide Examples and Connections

Give as many of your own personal examples as possible, as they will be very useful in supplementing and enriching the lecture. You can share examples from various students whom you may have worked with. You should be able to build a repertoire of examples as you facilitate more and more *Student LPI* workshops.

Also relate your presentation to the students' observations in their personal-best or most admired leader discussions, using the newsprint sheets that were created earlier.

Presentation of the *Student Leadership Practices Inventory* (20–40 MINUTES)

Explain the Instrument

Start by presenting the following explanation to the group:

> You will be receiving feedback from yourself (and from others) about how frequently you engage in those behaviors and actions that you (in your personal-best or most admired leader discussions) and Kouzes and Posner's research (as reported in *The Leadership Challenge*) have identified as the practices and behaviors of people when they are leading effectively and making a difference.
>
> The *Leadership Practices Inventory* was developed from the research of Kouzes and Posner on what people were doing when they were at their personal best as leaders. Kouzes and Posner translated the various actions, attitudes, tactics, and strategies into a set of statements about leadership behavior.
>
> They posed the following hypothesis:
>
> "If this is what people say they were doing when they were at their personal best as leaders, then we should expect to find that people who

engage in these behaviors are more effective and successful than people who do not engage in these behaviors."

Research over the years, now involving several hundred thousand people from a wide variety of organizations, offers empirical evidence to support this view.

Kouzes and Posner began extending their research to college students early on. They and their colleagues have worked with over 10,000 students, from junior high and high schools, community and junior colleges, four-year colleges and universities, and graduate schools. They spent nearly two years adapting the original *LPI,* which was developed for use with business and public-sector managers, into a version of the questionnaire that was appropriate for and in the language of students.

The *Student LPI* has been shown in a series of studies involving student leaders to differentiate successfully between effective and less effective student leaders, not only from their own personal perspectives, but also from the perspectives of their constituents (the members of their teams, clubs, or chapters, or the people living in their residence hall or working with them in their classes) and from the perspective of their university advisors and supervisors.

Ask Whether Everyone Completed the Instrument

Ask students if they have completed the *Student LPI-Self,* either at the start of the session or prior to the workshop and if they distributed copies of the *Student LPI-Observer* to their colleagues and had replies sent to the facilitator. Ask them to recall their small-group discussions about personal bests. Ask the students:

> In thinking back on the behavioral statements you responded to on the *Student LPI,* can you see how these emerged from experiences, like your own, of being at one's personal best as a leader?

> Are the behaviors and actions you discussed that you engaged in as leaders reflected in the *Student LPI* statements?

Discuss the Instrument's Development

Say a few words (or more, depending on the interest of the group) about the development of the *Student LPI* (Visual 3):

> The *Student LPI* contains thirty behavior-based statements. Each statement asks respondents about a specific leadership behavior and the extent to which respondents actually engage in that behavior. The *Student LPI* is not about attitudes or intentions but about actual behaviors.

The *Student LPI* provides information on each of the five leadership practices identified by Kouzes and Posner's research. There are six questions for each of the five leadership practices:

Model the Way
Inspire a Shared Vision
Challenge the Process
Enable Others to Act
Encourage the Heart

Briefly discuss the *reliability* and *validity* of the *Student LPI,* assuring the group that the *Student LPI* has been very thoroughly tested as a psychological instrument and is the leading leadership development instrument for use with students. The *LPI* is one of the leading leadership instruments for managers and executives as well. This is the first question in Chapter Two, Frequently Asked Questions About the *Student LPI,* of the *Student LPI Student Workbook.*

If you wish to go into detail about the concepts of reliability and validity, you could use the following script:

Reliability

Reliability refers to the extent to which the instrument contains measurement errors that cause scores to differ for reasons unrelated to the individual respondent. Reliability is determined empirically in several ways.

Internal Reliability

One way to determine reliability is to split the responses in half and test to see whether the two halves are correlated with one another. If the instruments were completed by the same person at the same time, we would expect responses to be reasonably consistent between the two halves. If they were perfectly independent (for example, one half is an apple, and the other half is an orange), we would expect zero correlation (although in the above example there might be some correlation, given that both items are fruits, rather than, say, a fruit and a vegetable). Should the halves be perfectly correlated (for example, two halves of the same apple) we would expect a 1.0 correlation coefficient. "Acceptable" scores are usually .50 or greater, and the *Student LPI* scales are generally above .66. The *Student LPI* has strong internal reliability.

Test-Retest Reliability

Another empirical measure of reliability is whether the instrument is overly sensitive to extraneous factors that might affect respondents' scores. For example, might the time of day, weather, individual personality, political or social events, internal organizational activity levels, or the like affect a respondent's scores from one administration of the instrument to another administration?

Over periods as short as one or two days or as long as three to four weeks, scores on the *Student LPI* show significant test-retest reliability (or consistency) at levels greater than a .91 correlation. However, it should be pointed out that we would expect *Student LPI* scores to change, assuming that respondents have attended a leadership workshop (such as this one), are consciously working to change their leadership behavior, or have experienced a significant life or organizational event.

Number of Items

Finally, reliability is enhanced when respondents are asked about an assessed behavior more than once. Therefore, a two-item scale is inherently more reliable than a one-item scale. The *Student LPI* scales each comprise *six* items or statements.

Validity

Validity is the determination of whether the instrument truly assesses what it purports to measure and also addresses the issue of "So what? What difference does it make how an individual scores on this instrument?" Like reliability, validity is determined in several ways.

Face Validity

The most common assessment of validity is called face validity. On the basis of subjective evaluation, does the instrument appear to be measuring what we think it is measuring? Given that the statements on the *Student LPI* are quite clearly related to the statements that you listed during the warm-up activities (personal best or most admired leader), we can say that the *Student LPI* has excellent face validity.

Empirical Measures

Validity is also determined empirically. Factor analysis is used to determine the extent to which the various instrument items are measuring common or different content areas. The results of these analyses consistently reveal that the *Student LPI* contains five factors and that the items within each factor correspond more among themselves than they do with the other factors. This means, for example, that the items that measure Challenge the Process are all more related (correlated) with one another than they are with items measuring the other four practices.

Predictive or Concurrent Validity

The question of "So what?" is probably the most important concern for you as workshop participants. To answer this question we look at determining predictive and/or concurrent validity, assessing the extent to which *Student LPI* scores are correlated (associated) with other important variables.

The *Student LPI* has excellent "So what?" validity, as shown by studies of the relationship between *LPI* scores and such variables as team cohesion, member commitment and loyalty, satisfaction, upward influence, and credibility.

For example, in studies of fraternity and sorority chapter presidents, effectiveness measured along several dimensions is positively correlated with the frequency with which these student leaders were seen as engaging in the *Student LPI* behaviors by chapter members. Resident directors reported that the most effective RAs on their campus were the ones who engaged most frequently in these leadership practices, and this was corroborated by assessments from the students living on their floors or in their facilities. New students on campus, participating in a three-day orientation session, reported levels of satisfaction that were positively correlated with the extent to which their orientation advisor engaged in these five leadership practices. Even the effectiveness of peer educators can be differentiated by the extent to which they behaved as leaders.

Overall, you can make a strong *normative* statement that those who engage in the set of behaviors described in the *Student LPI* more frequently, as opposed to less frequently, are more likely to be effective leaders. In fact, no matter where on the scale individuals initially score, to the extent that they can increase the frequency of their behavior along these dimensions, they will become more effective leaders.

If anyone has additional questions about reliability, validity, or the psychometric properties of the instrument, ask him or her to bring this up with you at the break.

Address Common Questions

You will want to address several frequently asked questions about the *Student LPI* (Visual 4):

Question 1: How reliable and valid is the Student LPI?

Generally, this is simply another way of asking the question, "Do my scores make a difference?" The answer is *yes*, there is a positive, direct correlation between *Student LPI* scores and effectiveness assessments. That is, as the frequency with which people are seen as engaging in the set of behaviors described on the *Student LPI* increases, so do positive assessments of such factors as their effectiveness, work group performance, team cohesiveness, credibility, and the like. Studies show that the *Student LPI* has very sound psychometric properties (which can be described more completely at the break—unless many people are interested in the research).

Question 2: What are the right answers?

There are no universal right answers when it comes to leadership. Still, the research indicates that the more frequently you are perceived as engaging in the behavior and actions identified in the *Student LPI,* the more likely it is that you will be perceived as an effective leader.

Question 3: Should my perceptions be consistent with the ratings other people give me?

The general answer to this question is *yes*, although there may be understandable exceptions, which we will discuss more when we look at the actual data. The usual response is that people are more effective when their self-perceptions match the perceptions of them provided by other people.

Question 4: Can I change my leadership behavior?

To this question the answer is categorically *yes*. Leadership is a skill like any other skill, which means that, with feedback, practice, and good coaching, people can improve at it. However, few people improve their skills dramatically overnight!

Score and Interpret the *Student LPI* (30–60 MINUTES)

The following steps presume that students have responses not only from their own instruments but also from the *Student LPI-Observer*. If data is available only from the *Student LPI-Self*, suggest (1) that they be aware of the tendency to rate themselves higher than others do and (2) that the most important perceptions are those from the people whom they are trying to influence and lead. Still, much can be learned from an analysis of one's self-perceived strengths and areas for improvement.

In addition, these instructions describe the steps required for hand-scoring. If centralized or computerized scoring was used, please turn to Appendix E.

Turn to Scoring Grids

Having explained the leadership framework and assured the students that the *Student LPI* is a valid and useful instrument, direct students to pages 15 through 17 in their workbooks, which are the grids for recording *Student LPI* responses. You may also show Visual 5.

The first grid (Model the Way) is for recording responses for statements 1, 6, 11, 16, 21, and 26 from the *Student LPI-Self* and *Student LPI-Observer* instruments. These are the statements that relate to behaviors involved in Model the Way, such as finding your voice and setting an example. An abbreviated form of each statement is printed beside the grid as a handy reference.

Explain the Scoring Process

Ask the students to direct their attention to you for a few minutes while you explain how to record and interpret the data. Assure the group members that they will have individual time for further study and reflection on the feedback.

1. Transfer the Self and Observer Scores. Direct the students' attention to the section of the grid labeled "Self-Rating." Have them transfer their own responses to this first column. Remind them to use the columns (vertical) rather than the rows (horizontal).

If others were asked to complete the *Student LPI-Observer* and if the forms were returned, have them enter those scores in the columns (A, B, C, D, E, and so on) under the heading "Observers' Ratings" in the same way as the "Self-Rating" responses. The process is simply to transfer the numbers from page 4 of each *Student LPI-Observer* to the scoring grids. The grids provide space for the scores of as many as ten observers.

2. Total the Scores. After the students have recorded their responses for Model the Way, ask them to total each column and write the sums in the row marked "Totals."

Next have them add all the totals for observers—excluding the "Self-Rating" total—and enter their grand totals in the space marked "Total of All Observers' Scores" at the far right of the grid.

3. Average the Scores. Finally, to obtain their average scores, have each student divide his or her grand total by the number of people who completed the *Student LPI-Observer* for him or her and write this average in the "Average of All Observers" blank.

The sample that follows shows how the grid would look if responses for a Self and five Observers had been entered (Visual 5).

Sample Grid with Scores from Self and Five Observers

	SELF-RATING	OBSERVERS' RATINGS										
		A	B	C	D	E	F	G	H	I	J	
1. Sets personal example.	5	4	3	5	4	4						
6. Aligns others with principles and standards.	5	4	3	5	4	4						
11. Follows through on promises.	4	3	2	5	4	5						
16. Gets feedback about actions.	4	4	3	4	4	4						
21. Builds consensus on values.	5	4	3	5	4	5						TOTAL OF ALL OBSERVERS' SCORES
26. Talks about values and principles.	3	3	3	4	4	3						
TOTALS	26	22	17	28	24	25						116

TOTAL SELF-RATING: ___26___   AVERAGE OF ALL OBSERVERS: ___23.2___

4. Finish the Grids. Tell students to complete the other four grids in the same manner. The second grid (Inspire a Shared Vision) pertains to statements 2, 7, 12, 17, 22, and 27, which involve envisioning the future and enlisting the support of others. The third grid (Challenge the Process) pertains to statements 3, 8, 13, 18, 23, and 28, which involve searching for opportunities, experimenting, and learning from mistakes. The fourth grid (Enable Others to Act) pertains to statements 4, 9, 14, 19, 24, and 29, which involve fostering collaboration and strengthening others. The fifth grid (Encourage the Heart) pertains to statements 5, 10, 15, 20, 25, and 30, which involve recognizing contributions and celebrating values and victories.

Look at "Self" Scores

After everyone has finished recording scores, ask the students to begin looking at individual responses. Remind them of the rating system that was used:

"1" means that you *rarely or seldom* engage in the behavior.
"2" means that you engage in the behavior *once in a while*.
"3" means that you *sometimes* engage in the behavior.
"4" means that you engage in the behavior *often*.
"5" means that you engage in the behavior *very frequently or almost always*.

Have students begin to interpret their responses by examining their self-ratings. On each completed grid, have them look at their responses in the blanks marked "Total Self-Rating." Each of these totals represents the students' own responses to the six statements about one of the five leadership practices. Each total can range from a low of 6 to a high of 30.

Ask the students to write "1" to the left of the leadership practice with the highest total self-rating (in the "Self" column on page 19 of their workbooks), "2" by the next-highest total self-rating, and so on (Visual 6). Explain that this ranking represents the leadership practice with which he or she feels most comfortable, second-most comfortable, and so on.

Look at Observer Scores

Refer the students to the numbers in the blanks marked "Average of All Observers" on each grid. The number in each blank is the average score given by the people asked to complete the *Student LPI-Observer*. Like each total self-rating, this number can range from 6 to 30.

Have the students write "1" to the right of the leadership practice with the highest score (in the "Observers'" column on page 19 of their workbooks), "2" by the next-highest score, and so on. Explain that this ranking represents the leadership practice that others feel the student uses most often, second-most often, and so on (Visual 6).

Compare Self with Observer Rankings

Continue by asking students to next look at the relationship between the rank order of their self-ratings and the ratings of their observers. Tell them to think about the extent to which their self-perceptions are consistent with the perceptions of the people with whom they work and interact. Explain that you want them to disregard their absolute scores for a moment and to reflect on the match (or mismatch) between "self" and "observer" perceptions of "reality" (in terms of leadership).

Ask students:

Which of these two columns (Self or Observer) is the better representation of reality? If I didn't know you, but only had the *Student LPI* scores provided by you and by other people who had interacted with you, whose scores would I consider to be the better representation of how you actually behave?

The response from participants will generally be "the scores or assessments of others," and this is true. That is why it is important to look at the degree of agreement between the two rank orderings. Even though there may be differences between the absolute scores from the Self and Observer columns (that is, "26" is not the same as "23.2"), it is possible that both parties will agree on the rank order of this practice, indicating agreement on the strength of this leadership behavior versus the others.

Look at Each Question

Point out the columns marked with the letters "A," "B," "C," "D," and so on, noting that these represent the actual responses on The Five Practices from each person who completed the *Student LPI-Observer* (Visual 5). Tell the students that this gives them an overall assessment of their leadership practices as seen by each individual *Student LPI-Observer* respondent. Ask them to note where there is agreement and disagreement among these respondents about their strengths and areas for improvement in these leadership practices. Add the following:

The *Student LPI-Observer* respondents are not individually identified on your forms. People often wish they knew exactly who these individuals were so that they could better understand the feedback. Resist the desire to figure out the identities of particular individuals; it is more important that you understand what this person or these people are trying to tell you. In any case, earlier research has indicated that participants were only about 25 percent successful in matching names with scores.

The trade-off is generally between identification (nonconfidentiality) of respondents and quality of data. *Student LPI-Observer* respondents are more likely to give better (more honest, more candid) responses—positive as well as negative—when they don't have to worry about being identified. Kouzes and Posner have designed the questions to obtain the higher quality data. At the end of the workshop, several strategies will be offered to help you collect more data and find out more about people's opinions of your leadership effectiveness.

Graph the Scores

To compare *Student LPI-Self* and *Student LPI-Observer* assessments, refer students to the "Chart for Graphing Your Scores" on page 21 of their workbooks. You may also want to do an example on Visual 7 so that students can see what you are talking about. They can also refer to the example on page 20 of their workbooks. Instruct the students to chart their self-ratings on the five leadership practices (Model, Inspire, Challenge, Enable, and Encourage) by marking each of these points with a capital "S" (for "Self"), to connect the five resulting "S scores" with a *solid line,* and to label the end of this line "Self."

Next, have students chart the average observer scores by marking each of the points with a capital letter "O" (for "Observer"), to connect the five resulting "O scores" with a *dashed line,* and to label the end of this line "Observer."

Each student will now have a graphic representation (one solid and one dashed line) illustrating the relationship between his or her self-perception and the observations of other people.

- Direct their attention to how parallel the two lines are—indicating relative agreement about both strengths and areas for improvement.
- Point out that any significant gaps between Self and Observer ratings indicate areas for improvement.

Explain Percentiles. On the Chart for Graphing Your Scores (Visual 7), explain the column marked "Percentile." Say that percentiles represent the scores nationwide from students who have completed the *Student LPI-Self.* Give the following explanation:

Because scores are normally distributed (in the classic bell-shaped curve), most people's scores fall at the fiftieth percentile (roughly half of the scores fall above and roughly half of the scores fall below), and nearly two-thirds of all scores fall within one standard deviation of the mean.

A percentile ranking is determined by the percentage of people who score at or below a given number. For example, if a person's total self-rating for Model the Way is at the sixtieth percentile line on the chart, this means that this person assessed himself or herself higher than 60 percent of all people who have completed the *Student LPI*—this person ranked himself or herself in the top 40 percent in this leadership practice. Studies indicate that a "high" score is one at or above the seventieth percentile, a "low" score is one at or below the thirtieth percentile, and a score that falls between those ranges is considered "moderate."

Compare Scores with Those of Other Student Leaders. Ask the students, using these criteria, to circle "H" (for "High"), "M" (for "Moderate"), or "L" (for "Low") for each leadership practice in the "Range of Scores" table on page 22 of their workbooks (Visual 8). Have them compare their leadership scores (using the Percentile Rankings Chart, Visual 7) with those of other student leaders around the country. Remember that, given a normal distribution, it is expected that most people's scores will fall within the moderate range.

Give students a few moments to compare themselves normatively with other students. While this is interesting (and often requested by students), point out that this comparison does not necessarily say much about leadership for any particular person in any specific organization or organizational context. Explain by saying:

> Because leadership is a skill, you will want to determine what it will take for you to improve your base level of leadership ability regardless of where you are relative to others.

Optional: Facilitators should note that *Student LPI* data from some specific student populations are available in Appendix D: Comparative Data for the *Student LPI,* as well as on the website (www.theleadershipchallenge.com). While the data in the Percentile Ratings Chart is from *all* students, regardless of affiliation, it may at times be useful to look at the typical scores of students participating in particular organizational settings; for example, fraternity and sorority chapters, residence halls, orientation, student government, and the like. Armed with this information, a facilitator might be able to say something like, "It is interesting how fraternity leaders on our campus rate themselves in comparison with fraternity presidents at college campuses across the country."

Fill in Workbooks

Thus far you have been asking students to complete the analysis while you have been describing it. In a few moments you will give them some additional time to review the individual items on the *Student LPI* and to look more deeply at individual responses and specific items. Explain where in their workbooks they can make notes to themselves as they continue their analysis.

To facilitate individual assessment and interpretations, ask the students to look at the Exploring Specific Behaviors Within Leadership Practices section (pages 23–24) in their workbooks. Tell them that this space is provided for them to make notes to themselves about the *specific behaviors* within each leadership practice. For example, sometimes a student's score on a leadership practice may be high or low because *all* the specific behaviors were assessed as frequently, or as not frequently, engaged in. Other times the score may be influenced by only a single behavior or a few behaviors connected with a leadership practice. Here is where they can make notes about the specific behaviors that make up the various leadership practices and consider the opportunities for becoming better leaders.

For those students with data from Observers, the Comparing Observers' Responses section (page 25) provides space to note consistencies and inconsistencies between the assessments from their observers. They can examine this at the level of leadership practices as well as the specific behaviors within any one leadership practice. This is also a chance to identify any "outliers" among their observers and consider how it might be that one (or two) people see them so differently from everyone else on a specific behavior or overall leadership practice. Remind students that while they want to pay attention to the outlier respondent, they should not lose sight of the consistent responses from their other observers.

When they have completed this analysis, tell the students to summarize their findings by completing the Strengths and Opportunities Summary Worksheet on page 28 of their workbooks (Visual 9).

After completing the item-by-item analysis, looking at their own assessments in comparison with those provided by others, charting their scores against student leaders from across the country, and so on, students should be able to say about themselves: "Here's what I do well (or comfortably)" and "Here's an area where I could improve my leadership ability."

Provide students with sufficient time for both this analysis and summary. You can either have everyone in the group work until a specific time (or in the case of a class, this assignment could be taken home), and then provide instructions for completing the Action-Planning Worksheet (Visual 11; more details follow), or you can include instructions for action plans along with the preceding explanation for pages 30–31 of the workbook.

If you haven't taken a break yet, this is a perfect place to do so, and it is also a logical place to break if you are doing the Student LPI *over more than one session.*

Make Action Plans

Start by offering students some ideas for moving from analysis to action. Use Suggestions for Getting Started on Becoming a Better Leader (Visual 10), which is on page 29 of their workbooks. There are ten suggestions, two for each leadership practice, that are reasonable ways to get started on becoming a better leader. Say a word or two about each suggestion, providing an example or illustration. Depending on time, you could also brainstorm with the entire group about additional ideas. Alternatively, you could form small discussion groups to generate ideas, and then the small groups could share their ideas with the larger group.

In Appendix C of this *Facilitator's Guide* there are checklists with a number of additional suggestions for how students can improve their skills relative to each leadership practice. These checklists can be used in several ways:

- Make copies of the checklists as handouts for students. Distribute them prior to their action planning or later as further suggestions.
- Use the ideas from the checklists to supplement students' own brainstorming about how to improve their capabilities in these leadership practices.

> *Note:* We find it helpful to ask students to put a check mark by each suggestion that they think they could do *right away*. Then we suggest that students select one or two of the ideas that they checked and complete the Action-Planning Worksheet for how they will put these suggestions into practice in their organization (or club, group, team, community, project). Although students can use the ten suggestions immediately, you might recommend instead that they use these ideas as a starting point for brainstorming other ideas that will make even more sense for them in their own circumstances.

Add some of these to the ideas aired in the small group discussions about "What Works for Me" (see the next section).

- Make visuals or handouts of the checklists in Appendix C. Have students identify the items they think would be most useful, suggest variations on the ideas, and ask questions about how to implement any of the suggestions.

Fill in the Action-Planning Worksheet. Once you've finished "priming the pump" by giving students some suggestions and ideas for how they can be even better leaders than they are today, ask them to complete the Action-Planning Worksheet on pages 30–31 of their workbooks (Visual 11).

Encourage students to select at least one leadership practice or behavior that they believe they can improve and to create an action plan for doing so. The Action-Planning Worksheets also can be completed as a take-home assignment following the workshop or used as the basis for a follow-up leadership development program.

Note: The *Student LPI Student Workbook* contains one Action-Planning Worksheet. Students can copy the blank before filling it in, or just use separate sheets of paper to develop an action plan for each practice they want to improve.

Dyad or Triad Work   (10–30 MINUTES OR AS MUCH AS 90 MINUTES IF THE OPTIONAL ACTIVITY IS USED)

Students often find it helpful to share their scores with one another and to ask their peers for assistance in interpreting them. Peers often see messages not readily perceived by the recipient of the feedback. This peer exchange also helps students become more comfortable with openly discussing their strengths and areas for improvement. Going public increases ownership of the data and prepares them for back-home discussions they might wish to have with their constituents.

Hold Small-Group Discussions

Suggest that as students finish up their individual reflections they form small groups (perhaps at their tables) of two or three people.

Ask these small groups to discuss what sense they made of their feedback—what it told them about themselves, what actions they think they could take to improve themselves, and what information they wish they had to help them understand more clearly their *Student LPI* feedback.

Consider the Data

Following this discussion, provide students with a few more minutes to revisit their notes and make any additions based on any new input from the small group. They may also have some additional questions and insights they want to bring up with the entire group.

Optional Small-Group Activity   (30–60 MINUTES)

After providing students the opportunity to process their own data (which may or may not include completing the Action-Planning Worksheets), you may want them to think more about their leadership strengths and come up with suggestions for others.

Form Groups

Either put students into groups based on their most or second-most frequent leadership practice or, if you have access to the student's scores prior to the workshop, assign them to one of the five leadership practice groups. (This can also be done on a random assignment basis. Everyone has something to contribute for each leadership practice, even the one they claim to be the least comfortable or skillful with.)

Try to make the groups approximately equal in number of members. Keep the five breakout groups together in one room or assign them to different locations. Or give them the following assignment (below) to work together as a group outside of class and to be prepared to present their ideas at the next session of the class. Or have each member work on this assignment individually outside of class and to join their other group members at the next class session to produce a group's report on application ideas for the class.

Assign "What Works for Me"

Ask the members of each group to think about "what works for me" when it comes to using the particular leadership practice assigned to their group. (See the checklists in Appendix C, which can be used as visuals or as handouts.)

Have students take a few moments to jot down four or five ideas about how they personally use this leadership practice. Encourage them to be as specific as possible with their ideas, giving examples whenever they can.

When everyone has finished, have each group member share one idea from his or her list within the small group, continuing until all the ideas from each person are "in the air" (or "on the table"). The group members may want to talk more about these ideas with one another.

Have each group develop a list of eight to ten of their best ideas and write these on newsprint sheets or on an overhead transparency. Tell them that these are the ideas and suggestions the group would offer to others who want to be more effective in using this leadership practice.

After the groups come up with their lists, have them put stars by their two *best ideas,* which they will present orally to everyone else in the workshop. Make sure they choose a spokesperson for their group.

Present Ideas

Reassemble the five groups into one group. It doesn't matter which order the leadership practices are presented or discussed in (which is another observation about leadership that can be made).

Have each group post its entire list of ideas for its particular leadership practice. Have the spokesperson from each group explain their two best ideas to everyone else and provide examples of how to implement them (for those who may be less comfortable in doing so, or who may not know how).

Tell each spokesperson to think of his or her job in this presentation as coaching the rest of the group (or workshop participants or class) on how to become more comfortable and effective in using this leadership practice. The goal is that everyone in the workshop will end up with a number of practical ideas for improving his or her leadership abilities.

Record the Results

When each spokesperson is done, ask if anyone in that group wants to make any additional comments or if anyone in any of the other groups has any questions or needs any clarification (for example, sometimes something else will be written on the newsprint that needs an explanation). (*Note:* The checklists in Appendix C can also be handed out at this point.)

After the five group presentations (one for each leadership practice), the newsprint sheets from this exercise can be collected, transcribed, and copies can be made for each students' leadership "tool kit."

(If the exercise is given as a take-home assignment, instruct each group to bring sufficient copies of its newsprint or overhead transparency or Power-Point presentation for everyone else in the workshop or class.)

Wrap Up the Discussion

Following the presentations, give students some time to make notes about the lessons learned from this coaching session. Ask them:

> Given these presentations and applications ideas, what else can you do to be an even better leader?

Sharing the *LPI* Feedback with Constituents (OPTIONAL; 10–20 MINUTES)

This section presumes that feedback from the *Student LPI-Observer* is available.

Think Ahead

Remind students that leadership is a relationship—that without constituents there is no leader—and explain that one of the most important ways to benefit from the *Student LPI* feedback is to share both the results and tentative interpretations with the people who provided or generated the data in the first place.

To reinforce the importance of students incorporating the *Student LPI* feedback into their back-home lives, have them think for a few minutes about how they are going to share their feedback, interpretation, and action plans with their constituents.

Explain that it is these people who can also help to clarify ambiguous or inconsistent scores. In addition, gaining their support will make any leadership development effort that much more painless and any experiments more likely to be successful.

Gain Commitment

Accomplish the first step in this process by having all students make a commitment to hold such a feedback session with their constituents following the workshop. Have each student choose a time when he or she will hold such a meeting (even if it is one-on-one) and whom he or she will invite to attend and participate in the dialogue.

Confirm in Writing

If time permits, have students actually write out what they will say to others about what they have learned, what they were delighted or surprised about, what they plan to do in the future, and the like.

Tell the students that what they do in their back-home situations with the information they have about their leadership styles is an important opportunity to put the entire leadership model that they have been learning about into practice. Tell them the following:

Since most of us, especially those in leadership positions, don't typically share feedback with others, the act of doing so is an example of our willingness to Challenge the Process by experimenting and taking a risk. In having this conversation, you also create an opportunity to Inspire a Shared Vision by talking about the things that are most important to you (vision and values) and to your organization (or club, team, or whatever applies) and both why and how these things are important to everyone in the organization as well. By letting others know that their opinions are taken seriously, you Enable Others to Act and underscore how competent and influential you find others to be. Handling constructive criticism as well as praise when you discuss your leadership style with others requires that you Model the Way. Finally, you can Encourage the Heart by thanking people for taking the time to give you feedback, and even provide doughnuts and coffee for the discussion!

Moreover, within this session (which might be facilitated by a third party such as a faculty or student services advisor), you can gain considerable insight into how your actions are perceived (perhaps differently from how they are intended) and ideas about what others believe you could be doing more of, better, or even less of ("stop doing. . .").

If time permits in the workshop (or class), provide some opportunity for students to pair-up or form small groups with several of their peers and to share their Action Plans. Perhaps their colleagues may be able to provide some helpful suggestions for accomplishing some of these tasks and/or pitfalls to avoid. This small group might also discuss the actions of group members that disenable them from being better leaders, and how these might be positively addressed.

Dispel Fears

If students are uncomfortable with the thought of reviewing their *Student LPI* feedback in a group setting, encourage them to consider doing this one-on-one or with small clusters of people, beginning with those with whom they have the best relationships.

Workshop Closing (5 MINUTES)

As you bring the workshop to closure, you have an important opportunity not only to summarize what has gone on but to encourage students to continue to take on the *challenge* of being leaders and of being even better leaders than they have been. Share some of the following observations and add your own hints to help and encourage students to develop into exemplary leaders:

No single instrument is a perfect measure or a perfect predictor of behavior. Although the *Student LPI* is a valid and reliable inventory, it does not describe the entire universe of leadership. Continually seek other useful, valid, and reliable sources of feedback.

The best way to find out what others mean by the scores or ratings they gave is to ask them. Rather than trying to second-guess the people who have completed the *Student LPI-Observer* for you, have one-on-one discussions with each of these people or arrange a group meeting to openly discuss the scores and ask for information on why certain responses were given. Doing so requires a certain degree of trust between you and your constituents, but if that trust exists, these discussions are the most beneficial way of finding out additional information about your leadership practices and effectiveness.

Leadership development is self-development. Leaders are their own instruments—their success and effectiveness depend on how finely tuned and well practiced they are. The only way to become a better leader is to participate continually and actively in your own development.

6

Design and Follow-Up Options

Use the *Student LPI-Observer*

If students have not yet done so, encourage them to use the *Student LPI-Observer* to gather feedback on other people's perceptions of their leadership practices. The perceptions of other people can be invaluable to students making developmental plans as leaders. Students who have already solicited feedback from members of their organizations can gather data from people outside of their organizations—alumni, university officials, and faculty, as well as peers who are in comparable positions.

Collect Open-Ended Feedback

Attach an open-ended feedback sheet to the *Student LPI-Observer* to allow students to gather more prescriptive information specific to their own situations. Respondents who are concerned about anonymity can usually prepare their feedback on a personal computer and print out an unidentifiable response page. Following are examples of questions that have been used for the open-ended section:

- Looking back over the individual statements in the *Student LPI*, which five behaviors do you wish this person would engage in more frequently? Please list them by number. Why are these important?
- Think about how you would describe this person's characteristics (personal values, traits, attributes) to someone else. What adjectives would you use?
- What does this person need to do to improve his or her abilities to lead?

Offer Additional Workshops

Offer a workshop on each one of The Five Practices. Students can select those practices they would like to improve and participate in the relevant workshop. With assistance, student leaders might also take responsibility for designing and facilitating such additional workshops.

Have a Team-Building Session

Offer a team-building session that includes members of the students' organizations. The student leaders can use their feedback on the *Student LPI* as a portion of the meeting. The whole team could be asked to complete the *Student LPI-Observer* and discuss their perceptions with the student leader. A team-building session can be designed around the ideas contained in *The Leadership Challenge*.

Show *The Leadership Challenge* Video

The Leadership Challenge video (about 27 minutes) provides an overview of the Kouzes-Posner leadership framework. This can be used in the *Student LPI* feedback workshop or subsequent workshops to illustrate the Five Practices of Exemplary Student Leadership®.

Viewers will observe the actions of various leaders: a Farm Credit Services of America vice president changing employees' reactions to performance appraisals; a Stanford University student development director preparing students for community service; the CEO of newly merged and morale-burdened Sinai-Grace Hospital turning things around; the Regen Technologies CEO empowering a committee of workers to choose a new employee health insurance plan; and a senior manager at FedEx exploring how to keep staff excited and interested. Each of these remarkable leaders moves structures and staff—and themselves—from ordinary to extraordinary. This video is available through CRM Learning (800-421-0833 or www.crmlearning.com).

Form Developmental Partnerships

Ask students to form partnerships of two or three people and set an agenda for where they would like to go next in their development as leaders. As partners, students are expected to support one another in their efforts, through both encouragement and counsel. A number of interesting and practical developmental suggestions are provided at the end of Chapters Three through Twelve in *The Leadership Challenge*. (You can view and/or download the Instructor's Guidebook in the Information for College and University Instructors section at www.theleadershipchallenge.com.) Ask each member of the partnership to make a commitment to complete one or two developmental actions within the month following the workshop and have partners set a specific date to meet again to review their progress, learn from one another's efforts, and celebrate their accomplishments.

Use *The Student Leadership Planner*

Let students know about *The Student Leadership Planner.* The Planner was designed to be a step-by-step guide to helping students use The Five Practices of Exemplary Student Leadership® to continue meeting their leadership challenges and further develop their leadership abilities. It is intended to be used after students have already completed the *Student Leadership Practices Inventory.* It begins by having students review the Action Plans they identified as part of the development feedback from the *SLPI* and what they learned about leading from that experience. We believe that *The Student Leadership Planner* will enable students to continue growing and developing themselves as leaders on their own.

RECOMMENDED READING

Model the Way

Abrashoff, D. M. (2002). *It's your ship: Management techniques from the best damn ship in the Navy.* New York: Warner Books.

Block, P. (2003). *The answer to how is yes: Acting on what matters.* San Francisco: Berrett-Koehler.

Heifitz, R. A., and Linsky, M. (2002). *Leadership on the line: Staying alive through the dangers of leading.* Boston: Harvard Business School Press.

Kouzes, J. M., and Posner, B. Z. (2003). *Credibility: How leaders gain and lose it, why people demand it.* San Francisco: Jossey-Bass.

Parker, P. J. (2000). *Let your life speak: Listening to the voice of vocation.* San Francisco: Jossey-Bass.

Inspire a Shared Vision

Bennis, W., Spreitzer, G. M., and Cummings, T. G. (Eds.). (2001). *The future of leadership: Today's top leadership thinkers speak to tomorrow's leaders.* San Francisco: Jossey-Bass.

Clarke, B., and Crossland, R. (2002). *The leader's voice: How communication can inspire action and get results.* New York: Select Books.

Maxwell, J. C. (2002). *Developing the leader within you* (2nd ed.). New York: Nelson Books.

Pearce, T. (1995). *Leading out loud.* San Francisco: Jossey-Bass.

Wheatley, M. (2002). *Turning to one another: Simple conversation to restore hope to the future.* San Francisco: Berrett-Koehler.

Challenge the Process

Farson, R., and Keyes, R. (2002). *Whoever makes the most mistakes wins: The paradox of innovation.* New York: The Free Press.

Hamel, G. (2002). *Leading the revolution: How to thrive in turbulent times by making innovation a way of life*. London: Plume Books.

Peters, T. (1999). *The circle of innovation: You can't shrink your way to greatness*. New York: Vintage Books.

Semler, R. (2004). *The seven-day weekend: Changing the way work works*. New York: Portfolio/Penguin Group.

Yamashita, K., and Spataro, S. (2004). *Unstuck: A tool for yourself, your team, and your world*. New York: Portfolio.

Enable Others to Act

Blanchard, K., Carlos, J., and Randolph, W. A. (1999). *The three keys to empowerment*. San Francisco: Berrett-Koehler.

Cherniss, C., and Goleman, D. (Eds.). (2001). *The emotionally intelligent workplace: How to select for, measure, and improve emotional intelligence in individuals, groups, and organizations*. San Francisco: Jossey-Bass.

Lencioni, P. M. (2002). *The five dysfunctions of a team: A leadership fable*. San Francisco: Jossey-Bass.

O'Reilly, C., and Pfeffer, J. (2000). *Hidden value: How great companies achieve extraordinary results with ordinary people*. Boston: Harvard Business School Press.

Stack, J., and Burlingham, B. (2003). *A stake in the outcome: Building a culture of ownership for the long-term success of your business*. New York: Currency.

Encourage the Heart

Blanchard, K., and Bowles, S. (2000). *High five! The magic of working together*. New York: William Morrow.

Cameron, K. S., Dutton, J. E., and Quinn, R. E. (Eds.). (2003). *Positive organizational psychology: Foundations of a new discipline*. San Francisco: Berrett-Koehler.

Deal, T., and Deal, M. K. (1998). *Corporate celebrations: Play, purpose, and profit at work*. San Francisco: Berrett-Koehler.

Kouzes, J. M., and Posner, B. Z. (1998). *Encouraging the heart: A leader's guide to rewarding and recognizing others*. San Francisco: Jossey-Bass.

Ventrice, C. (2003). *Make their day! Employee recognition that works*. San Francisco: Berrett-Koehler.

APPENDIX A

Recalling a Personal-Best
Leadership Experience

We have learned from our leadership research that *experience is the best teacher.* Most people learn what to do from trying it themselves or watching others. We believe it is important to base our leadership practices on the *best* experiences, those times when we or others do our absolute *personal best.*

Take a few moments to write down some notes about your personal-best leadership experience. Don't worry. There is no competition about whose experience is best or whether this is some all-time best. You will be sharing your experiences with others in a small group, exploring the behaviors and actions that make a difference. Here's how to proceed:

1. Briefly describe the context of this situation or experience.

   _____

   _____

   _____

   _____

   _____

   _____

   _____

2. List the five to seven most important actions or behaviors you took as a leader in this situation. In other words, what things did you do as a leader that made a difference in this situation? (Use the other side of this page as needed.)

   _____

   _____

   _____

   _____

   _____

   _____

Sample Student Responses to the Assignment: Recalling a Personal-Best Leadership Experience

Facilitators may find these case studies useful in supplying additional examples of students at their personal best as leaders.

Mindy Behse

Looking back, one of my best and most memorable leadership experiences was in my junior and senior years in high school when I was the captain for our swim team. Usually the captain was a senior; however, my junior year I was elected by my teammates. I had no idea my teammates saw me as a potential leader, especially as a junior. I took on the responsibility with enthusiasm.

I think I was able to lead the team and make a difference because I consistently encouraged others to keep trying and told them their participation was all that mattered. Swimming takes a lot of motivation. I was aware of this and tried to inspire those who lacked some self-motivation. I did this by positive reinforcement and complimenting those individuals who did a good job or who improved just a little.

Another way I was able to motivate my teammates was to tell those who missed a practice that I missed them. Therefore they felt like they were needed and appreciated. Being a good captain and leader included setting a good example. For instance, I was not late for practice nor did I miss a practice. I also worked hard during workouts and worked with the coach, not against him. Other duties included organizing team parties, leading cheers, and making sure everyone was informed about when the meets were and what time practice started.

Another reason why I had a successful leadership experience had to do with setting goals for the team. At the beginning of the season I rallied everyone together and discussed what our team wanted to accomplish that year. Some of our goals included placing in the top three in our division and sending at least seven swimmers to state.

Sherrie Buente

During my senior year in high school, I was captain of our school's soccer team. I believe that at this time I was at my personal best.

I was able to challenge the process when our coach (unusual as it may seem) would give us too many days off and not practice us enough. I would get the girls together for fun practices, even if it was just to pass the ball around. Also, we would have team meetings called by the captains and players only after we lost, which was not often, and we would discuss our downfall and mistakes so that we could learn from them.

I enabled others to act by allowing the team to make decisions about what activities we were going to do and other sorts of decisions that a captain might normally have made.

I was really able to model the way with this group of girls because I was one who ended up being recruited to play college soccer. They could see that was my style and that is what I expected from them. I feel I inspired a shared vision by always being positive from the captain's position. Also, every time before the game our team would sit in a circle and each person would say something positive about the upcoming game. We even would do this right on the field in front of the fans!

And last, I encouraged the heart by always telling my teammates how proud I was of each of them when we were doing something good, and even when something went wrong. Also, I held a team lunch one day before a big game and brought them each a red rose (our school color) before our first playoff game. That year we won our league (undefeated) and made it to the state playoffs. I would like to think it was because I helped out in the leadership role in addition to the fine talent we had on the team.

Francine Cruz

One of my best memories of being a leader was when I was in charge of our floor flag-football team freshman year. I had to gather all the girls on our floor and get them together for practices and games. It was fun because it gave us all a chance to get to know each other better and brought our floor as a whole closer together.

I think that some of the things that made this a good leadership experience were: motivating the women on the floor to come to games, being supportive and always contacting them about concerns, always looking for ways to support and improve our team, and keeping everyone united— even when we had disagreements.

It was hard at first to motivate everyone to come out to practices and games, but I persisted. I tried to make practices fun and easy. It was more important to enjoy ourselves than to win. Even when we were losing, we still managed to have fun. When someone made a mistake, I did not get angry but tried to encourage her to do better next time.

There were times when it seemed that the team was splitting up into little groups. At those times, it became difficult, but I tried to remind them that we would win together and separating would only harm the team.

This leadership experience was fun because I learned that keeping a group of people united is difficult and that being supportive and a team player was important.

Annya Dushine

I was at my personal best as a leader when I worked as a choreographer for a dance team at a summer camp. I displayed many important leadership qualities because the girls were depending on me for help and to make them the best. Some qualities I had as a leader were:

1. I motivated and inspired each girl to do her best by setting an example and constantly reminding her of reward.

2. I organized everything and looked for ways to improve.
3. I always searched for new ideas in order to make it more interesting and exciting for the girls so as not to lose their motivation.
4. I was open-minded and listened to what each girl had to input.
5. I made everyone feel that they were doing their best and never put anyone down or made them feel inferior.
6. I focused on each individual's strengths and brought that out in everyone.
7. Most importantly, I made it fun!!!

Ignacio Guerrero

One specific time in which I think I was at my personal best as a leader was when my mother passed away on New Year's Day. She was terminally ill with Hepatitis C and had been slowly fading away and getting weaker day by day. Most of my family members had tried to prepare themselves for the inevitable, but when the time came on the first of January at 10:10 P.M., despite how prepared we thought we were, we still were not ready to let my mom go. That was when I feel I was at my personal best as leader.

After my mom passed away, I took on the responsibility of calling 911 and reporting her death due to terminal illness. When the police arrived, most of my family members were pretty shaken up due to what had just occurred. So when the police officers arrived, I greeted them and, in a calm and collected manner, gave them all the information they needed to fill out a report. My brothers and sisters saw how I was handling the situation and that is when I believe I became a leader. I think that my calm behavior at a very emotional time in my family's life gave my brothers and sisters emotional strength and motivated them to act "strong" in support of each other.

Seven actions I think contributed to my personal-best leadership experience were

- Behaving confidently in my actions
- Being flexible in a demanding situation
- Supporting
- Motivating my other family members
- Inspiring others
- Acting honestly (behaving normal in an abnormal situation)
- Concentrating on my major strength at that moment (that my mother was not suffering any longer)

Robert Laubach

It was just after Christmas in my junior year of high school when I realized the commitment I had made as junior class president. At this time the preparation, construction, delegation, and organization for the school's Valentine formal dance and the junior prom needed to really get rolling, and it was my responsibility to make this happen. The actions I took and the end result of those following several months became one of my personal-best experiences as a leader.

My first of many decisions was to give focus to the many lofty ideas for these big events. This required me to cut and paste all the input I was receiving from the student body into a feasible goal. I absolutely love construction projects; therefore once we as class officers chose a topic, I immediately was ecstatic about the possibilities and how I could find practical ways of making it work. My task-oriented mentality began figuring out how to accomplish these goals. I worked very well with the art teacher at my school, and together we set the vision. It was my responsibility to delegate the work.

Being president made it easy for me to ask people to help. However, I did find that large projects often overwhelm people. Therefore I learned quickly to communicate our ideas by giving lots of people several little related tasks. This part of the production was fun because I found, if I gave each person the general purpose of their task and encouraged their creativity and work, they completed their task better than anticipated. Because I oversaw the entire project and knew the goal, I acted as a mediator to see that all these pieces fit together. I worked very hard on the project and took on the details that everyone else discouraged as too hard. (I actually constructed life-size 3D animals, fifteen-foot tall freestanding arches, etc. I tend to think big.)

As an "elected leader" I often found myself as a sort of peacemaker, trying to keep everyone focused on the project rather than the bickering that occurs when lots of things need to be done. This project took all my energy and enthusiasm; it is clear to me that had I not been dedicated to the task I would have made a poor leader. Everyone involved was very proud of the final product. As a leader it was very rewarding to take these scattered ideas and see them converted to a complete and enjoyable product.

Bob Lee

I remember the time when I was in high school, and I was chosen by my peers to be one of the organizers of a charity drive that would help underprivileged children. The charity drive was a lot of hard work and very time-consuming; yet I had many ideas to raise funds. I felt important to the group and had control over many activities.

As the leader, I had to motivate and inspire my friends and others to participate in the charity drive, if they knew about the worthy cause. I motivated and inspired my friends by talking to them about the helplessness of the children and appealed to their compassion.

I was responsible for planning the activities and thinking of new ideas for raising money. I had to be creative and to explore new possibilities. I wanted to bring the group's unique abilities together and make the charity drive a success. Since each person had a special talent, I knew some people would be better suited to doing certain tasks. I tried to get them to follow my instructions, but many of them would improvise and even improve on what I instructed them to do.

I had to be the example of the group, for I worked hard and was determined to make the charity drive a success. I wanted everyone to follow my lead and accomplish their assigned tasks. I was the center of all the activities. I was always there if anyone had any questions or ideas because I enjoyed suggestions and was always looking for ways to improve. Many of their suggestions I used because they would improve the charity drive.

I was supportive and commended anyone who did a good job or accomplished a task because I knew we were a team. I wanted everyone to be involved and make a contribution. I loved constructive criticism and would be grateful for all the help I could get.

My goal of the charity drive was to make it a huge success and raise funds for the underprivileged children, which I tried to do. I maintained the goal and had a great charity drive that raised a lot of money. As I look back on the experience, I accomplished the goal and learned many things. I learned I can work with others and have authoritative responsibilities. I was understanding of any problems and handled myself well when pressured to perform. I felt as if I was the leader and was astounded by my abilities.

David Mvilenbing

Organizing a summer camping trip for a group of twenty people was my personal-best leadership experience. I successfully created a camping trip with my closest friends, with all the organizational aspects and leadership implicitly given to me.

Examples of modeling the way:

- I was actively involved in all aspects that my group was working on, constantly checking on and advising my friends to make sure all would be ready. I was able to focus on the necessities for a successful camping trip, but not eliminating all the fun items too.

Examples of inspiring a shared vision:

- I told stories of past camping trip failures and successes, along with sharing with my group forecasts of the fun and success we would face if we stayed organized.

Examples of challenging the process:

- I didn't let anyone influence my decisions, and did the whole thing on my own. Because this was about six years ago, when I was sixteen, I feel that this was a big risk not relying on my parents' help.

Examples of enabling others to act:

- I let other members of the group do certain assigned tasks for me, because I didn't want any duplicate items brought, and I couldn't afford or didn't have time to bring everything necessary for a fun camping trip myself.

Examples of encouraging the heart:

- I guess I was able to show my friends how working hard and staying organized can result in a successful trip. I got my group excited about the trip, with a promise of good times. And did we ever celebrate. And the trip went beautifully.

Jeremy Shelley

A time when I was probably at my personal best was when I coached CYO basketball for four years. As a coach I tried to do everything I could to be a leader and get the most out of the kids on the team. We were very successful because of the accomplishments on the basketball court, with one loss being the worst year in my four years of coaching.

Some of the different techniques I tried to use as a leader included, among others, motivation. Motivation is one of the keys to get people to work hard and accomplish the leader's task. I also tried to be supportive and keep in close touch with the kids, which also helped. I created a goal and a vision for the team that they could strive for and try to achieve. The vision was to win and have fun while at it. I placed myself at the center, along with the other coaches, and everything revolved around us.

I looked for ways to improve the skills and abilities of the players and the team as a whole so that we could be better each and every time we played. Finally, I tried to search for ways and ideas to do anything I could to benefit the team, whether it was a new play or a new drill. These are some of the concepts a leader should exhibit, and if used properly he or she will be successful.

Bryan Smart

The time I was at my personal best as a leader was when I played on my high school golf team my senior year:

1. I did my best to help all the players feel that they were important.
2. I would tell them that no matter how badly they were playing to just always do their best and never give up.
3. I told them all about my good and bad experiences and listened and learned from theirs.
4. I tried to give them self-confidence and a sense of pride in themselves.
5. The positions (or rather rank) of each individual team member did not matter because it was the total team score that counted, not the best (lowest).
6. Most important was for each one of us to believe in ourselves and credit ourselves for all the good things we did on the course and learn from the bad things and then forget about them.
7. Keeping focused through times of poor playing was also a major goal that I tried to push on to my teammates through my own actions and conduct/temperament.

APPENDIX B

Masters for Visuals and Handouts

The following pages are intended to be used as masters in creating overhead transparencies or handouts. The numbers on these masters (Visual 1A, 2A, and so on) correspond to those that appear in Chapter Five of this Facilitator's Guide (Workshop Process Details) and in Appendix E, which gives instructions about when and how to use these visuals in explaining the *Student LPI* and the computer-generated feedback reports.

Permission is hereby granted to project these visuals in workshops where the *Student LPI* is used and to photocopy them for use as overheads or handouts to participants in such workshops.

The Five Practices of Exemplary Leadership

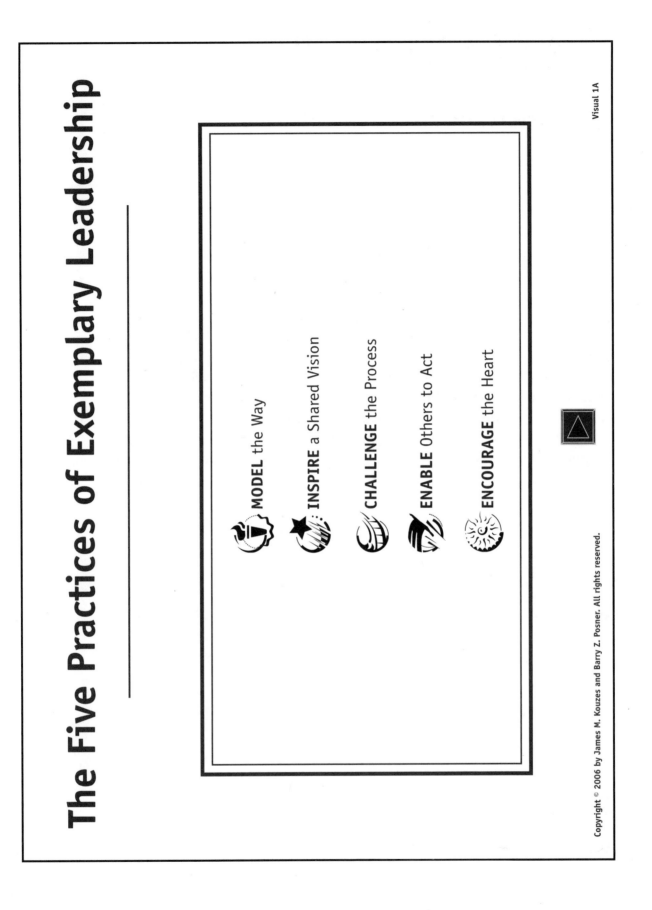

MODEL the Way

INSPIRE a Shared Vision

CHALLENGE the Process

ENABLE Others to Act

ENCOURAGE the Heart

MODEL the Way

Find your voice
by clarifying your personal values.

Set the example
by aligning actions with shared values.

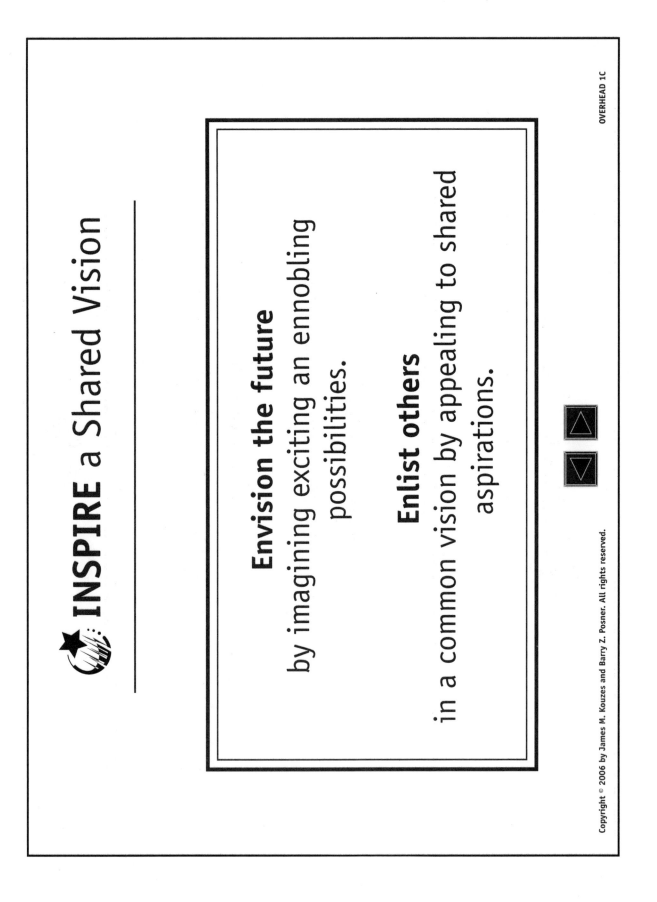

CHALLENGE the Process

Search for opportunities

by seeking innovative ways to change, grow, and improve.

Experiment and take risks

by constantly generating small wins and learning from mistakes

△ ▽

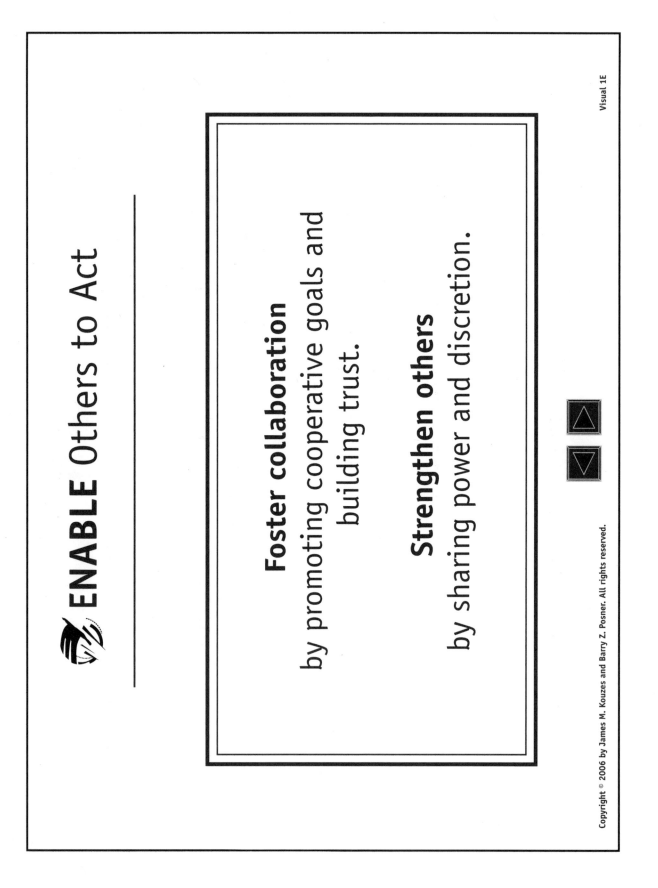

Visual 1E

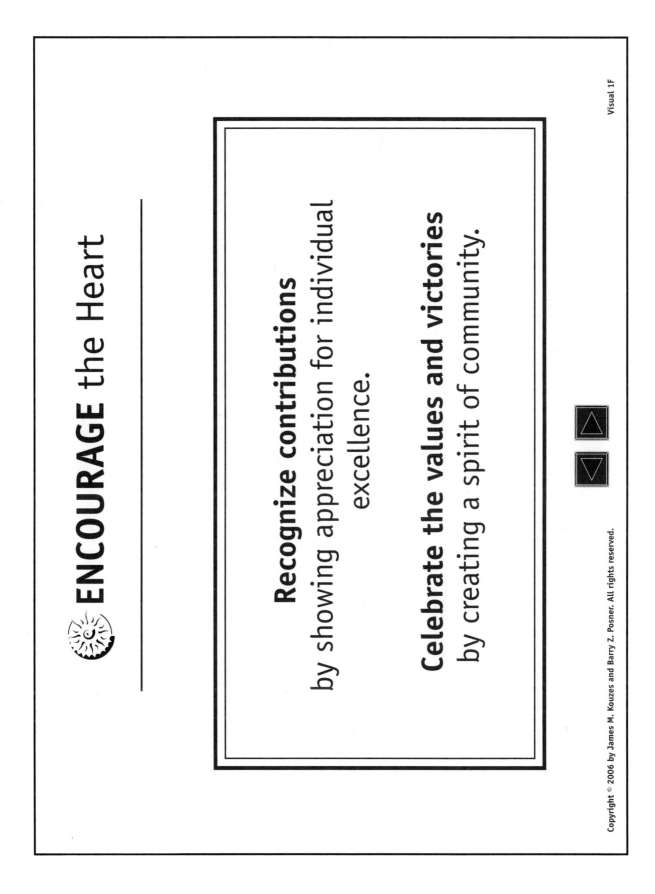

ENCOURAGE the Heart

Recognize contributions
by showing appreciation for individual excellence.

Celebrate the values and victories
by creating a spirit of community.

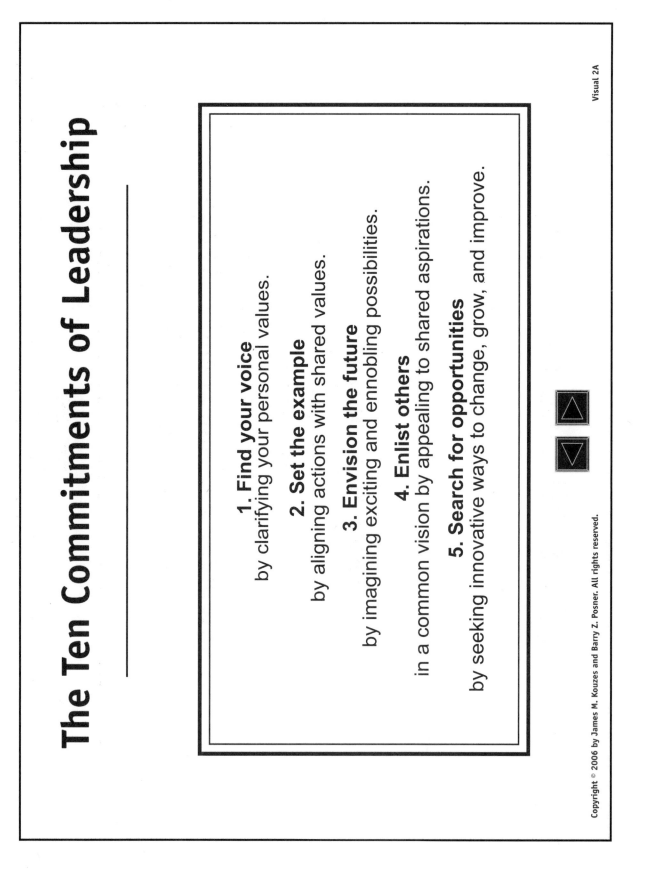

The Ten Commitments of Leadership

1. Find your voice
by clarifying your personal values.

2. Set the example
by aligning actions with shared values.

3. Envision the future
by imagining exciting and ennobling possibilities.

4. Enlist others
in a common vision by appealing to shared aspirations.

5. Search for opportunities
by seeking innovative ways to change, grow, and improve.

Visual 2A

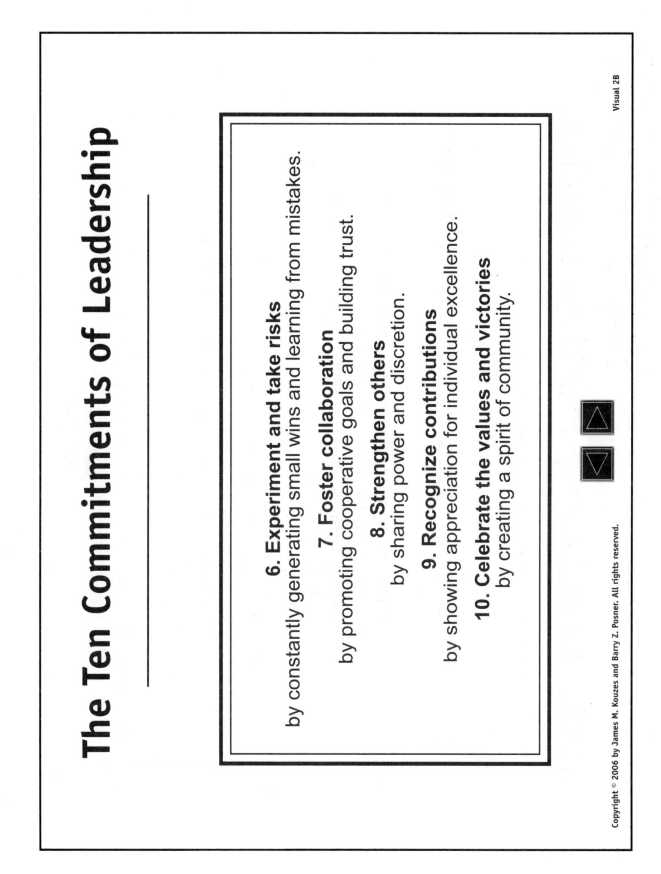

The Ten Commitments of Leadership

6. Experiment and take risks
by constantly generating small wins and learning from mistakes.

7. Foster collaboration
by promoting cooperative goals and building trust.

8. Strengthen others
by sharing power and discretion.

9. Recognize contributions
by showing appreciation for individual excellence.

10. Celebrate the values and victories
by creating a spirit of community.

Visual 2B

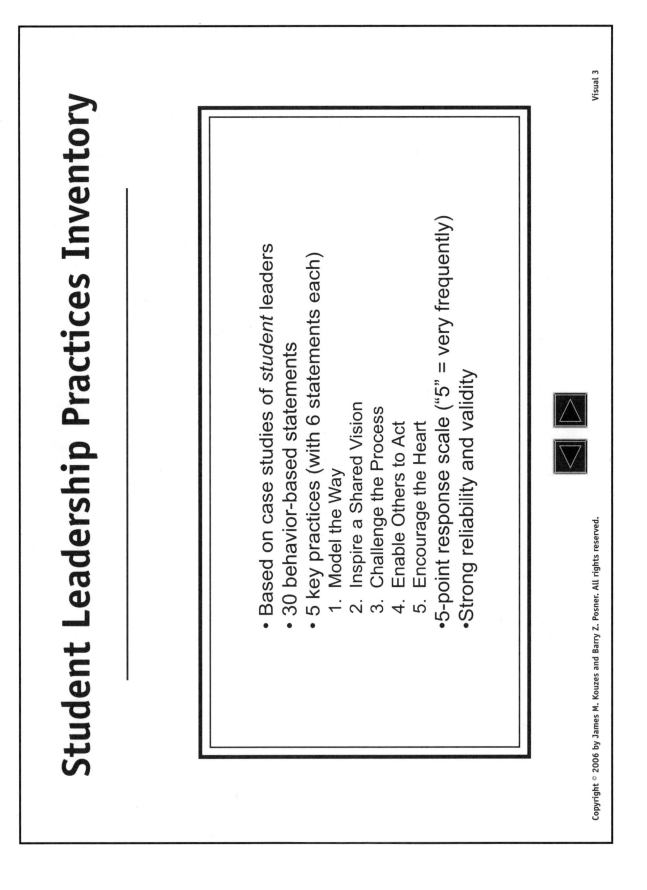

Student Leadership Practices Inventory

- Based on case studies of *student* leaders
- 30 behavior-based statements
- 5 key practices (with 6 statements each)
  1. Model the Way
  2. Inspire a Shared Vision
  3. Challenge the Process
  4. Enable Others to Act
  5. Encourage the Heart
- 5-point response scale ("5" = very frequently)
- Strong reliability and validity

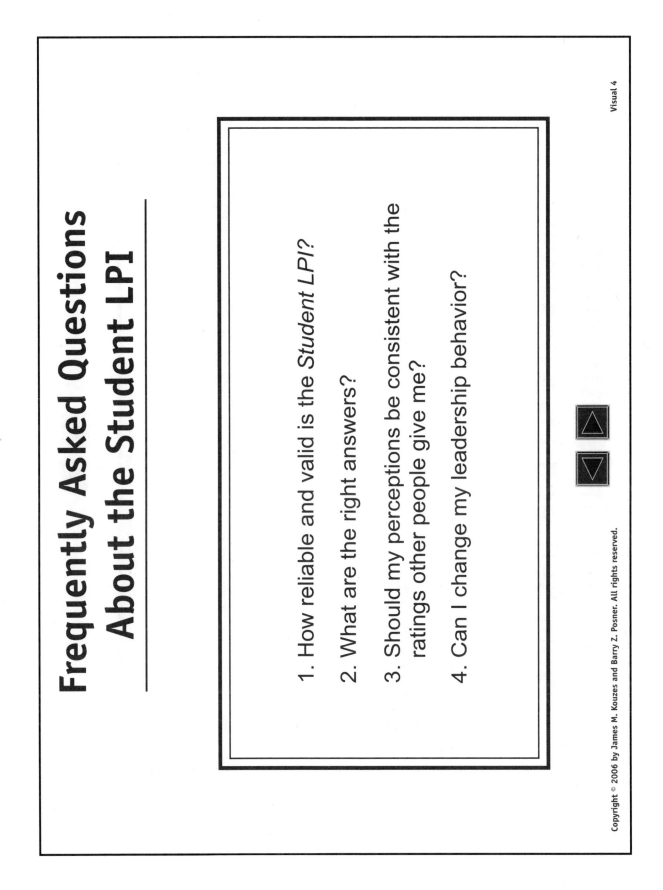

Frequently Asked Questions About the Student LPI

1. How reliable and valid is the *Student LPI?*

2. What are the right answers?

3. Should my perceptions be consistent with the ratings other people give me?

4. Can I change my leadership behavior?

Visual 4

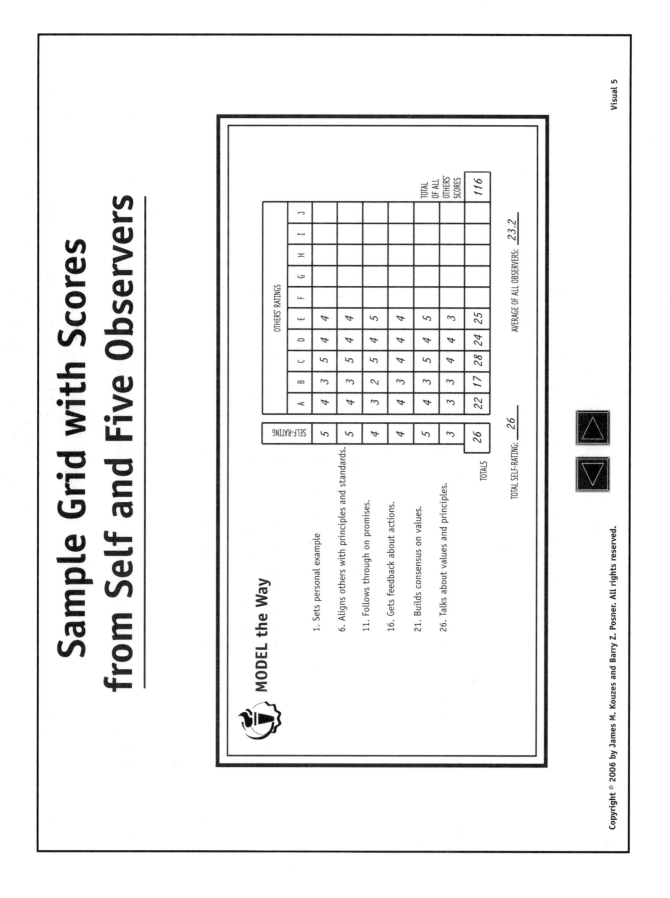

Sample Grid with Scores from Self and Five Observers

MODEL the Way

	SELF-RATING		A	B	C	D	E	F	G	H	I	J	
1. Sets personal example	5		4	3	5	4	4						
6. Aligns others with principles and standards.	5		4	3	5	4	4						
11. Follows through on promises.	4		3	2	5	4	5						
16. Gets feedback about actions.	4		4	3	4	4	4						
21. Builds consensus on values.	5		4	3	5	4	5						
26. Talks about values and principles.	3		3	3	4	4	3						
TOTALS	26		22	17	28	24	25						TOTAL OF ALL OTHERS' SCORES 116

OTHERS' RATINGS

TOTAL SELF-RATING: _26_   AVERAGE OF ALL OBSERVERS: _23.2_

Visual 5

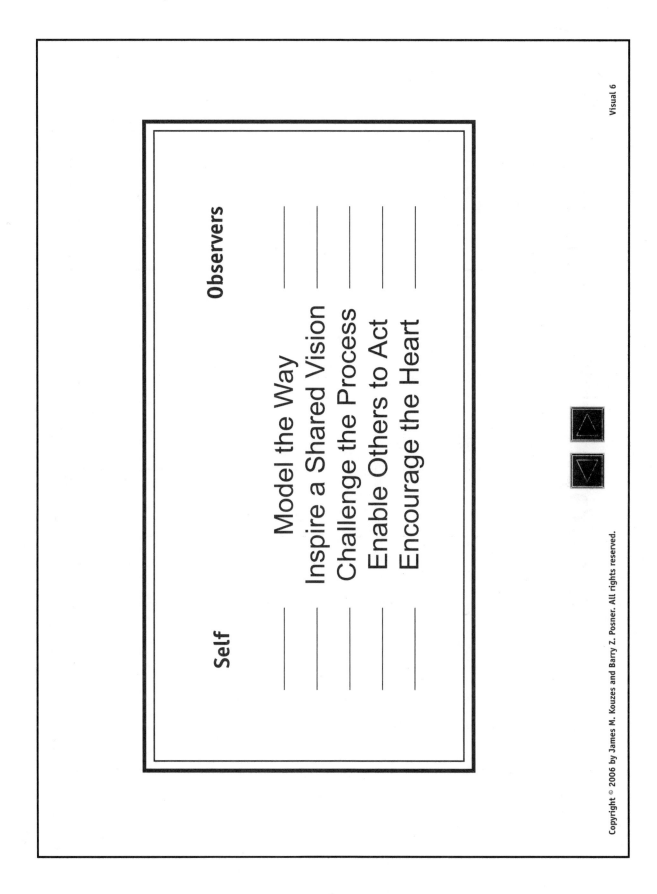

Visual 6

Chart for Graphing Your Scores

PERCENTILE		MODEL THE WAY	INSPIRE A SHARED VISION	CHALLENGE THE PROCESS	ENABLE OTHERS TO ACT	ENCOURAGE THE HEART
100	HIGH	•29	•29	•29	•29	•29
90		•28	•28	•28	•28	•28
		•27	•27	•27	•27	•27
80		•26	•26	•26	•26	•26
		•25	•25	•25		•25
70			•24	•24		•24
60	MODERATE	•24	•23	•23	•25	•23
		•23	•22	•22	•24	•22
50			•21	•21		
40		•22	•20	•20	•23	•21
30		•21		•19		
20	LOW	•20	•18	•18	•22	•20
		•19	•17	•17	•21	•19
10		•18	•16	•16	•20	•18
		•17	•15	•15	•19	•17
			•14	•14	•18	

Range of Scores

IN MY PERCEPTION		IN OTHERS' PERCEPTION	
PRACTICE	RATING	PRACTICE	RATING
Model the Way	H M L	Model the Way	H M L
Inspire a Shared Vision	H M L	Inspire a Shared Vision	H M L
Challenge the Process	H M L	Challenge the Process	H M L
Enable Others to Act	H M L	Enable Others to Act	H M L
Encourage the Heart	H M L	Encourage the Heart	H M L

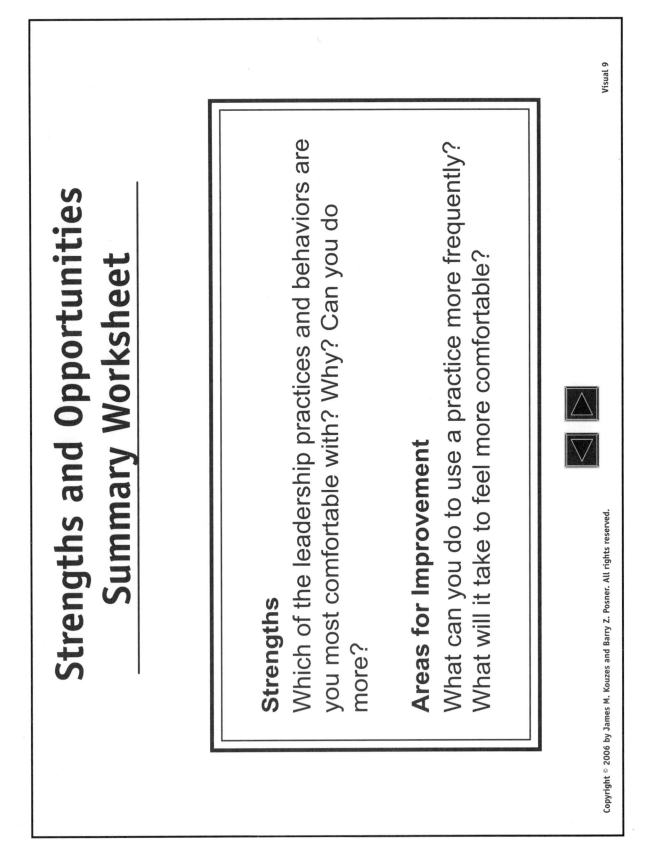

Strengths and Opportunities Summary Worksheet

Strengths

Which of the leadership practices and behaviors are you most comfortable with? Why? Can you do more?

Areas for Improvement

What can you do to use a practice more frequently? What will it take to feel more comfortable?

Visual 9

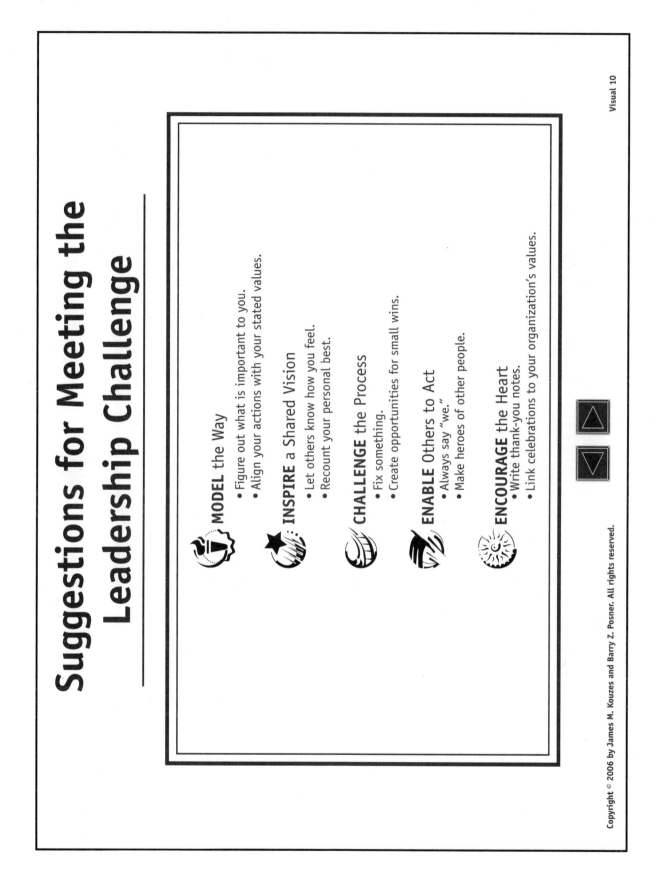

Suggestions for Meeting the Leadership Challenge

MODEL the Way
- Figure out what is important to you.
- Align your actions with your stated values.

INSPIRE a Shared Vision
- Let others know how you feel.
- Recount your personal best.

CHALLENGE the Process
- Fix something.
- Create opportunities for small wins.

ENABLE Others to Act
- Always say "we."
- Make heroes of other people.

ENCOURAGE the Heart
- Write thank-you notes.
- Link celebrations to your organization's values.

Visual 10

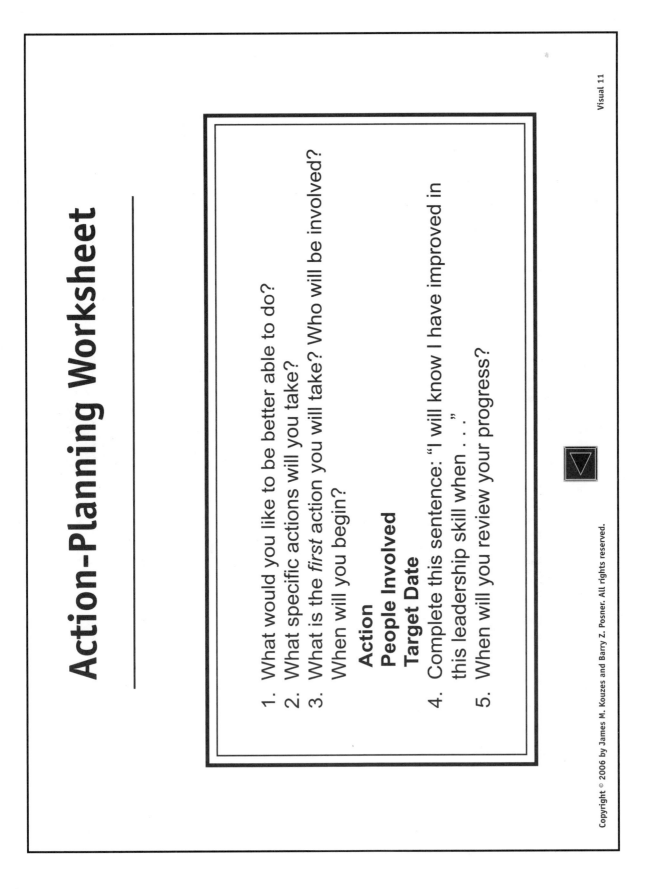

Action-Planning Worksheet

1. What would you like to be better able to do?

2. What specific actions will you take?

3. What is the *first* action you will take? Who will be involved? When will you begin?

   Action
   People Involved
   Target Date

4. Complete this sentence: "I will know I have improved in this leadership skill when . . . "

5. When will you review your progress?

Visual 11

APPENDIX C

Checklists of Actions for Meeting
the Leadership Challenge

Checklist for Model the Way

_____ Clarify your *personal credo*—the values or principles that you believe should guide your leadership behavior. Then talk about your credo with others in your organization (or team, club, class, community, program). Post this information prominently for everyone to see.

_____ Keep track of how you spend your time. Check to see whether your actions are consistent with what you and your colleagues have agreed is important. If you find inconsistencies, figure out what you need to do to align your actions with those values.

_____ Keep your daily planner or PDA at hand. Write down your promises as you make them. Review them daily and fulfill them on schedule.

_____ Develop a list of questions that you can ask at meetings to find out whether your team members are living out the team's values.

_____ Admit your mistakes. Say "I don't know." Show that you're willing to change your mind when someone comes up with a better idea.

_____ Make sure you wander around. Don't make people work to find you; go out and find them. Mingle. Just say "hi" and learn about what they are doing.

_____ Choose some people you consider to be role models. Learn whatever you can about them by reading biographies, watching films, interviewing, or spending some time with them.

_____ Visit a retail store that's widely acknowledged for its extraordinary customer service. Watch and listen to what store employees do and say. Interview a couple of the employees about how the store got such a stellar reputation. Apply these lessons to your own situation.

_____ Take a class in storytelling. Take a class in goal setting, on values clarification, on time management, or in active listening.

_____ Allow less experienced members to "shadow" you as you go about completing tasks and projects for your organization.

Checklist for Inspire a Shared Vision

_____ Envision yourself one year from now. Imagine that your organization (or club, team, group, community, project) has been named the outstanding group on campus. When you stand up at the award ceremony, what will you say about what you've done and why you did it?

_____ Visualize the possibilities. Focus on all the things that could happen correctly, not just the things that could go wrong.

_____ Write several positive affirmations: for example, "I'm confident that I'm finding opportunities as I accept these new challenges" or "I'm learning from my mistakes as I experiment with new ways to do things better."

_____ Meet with the people in your organization and ask them to talk about their hopes and aspirations for what this organization could be accomplishing. Make those common goals visible.

_____ Speak positively. Don't say _try,_ say _will._ Sure, there are lots of reasons why this or that might not happen, and of course it will be hard work, but people don't get charged up when you're tentative and noncommittal.

_____ Make the intangible tangible. Slogans, theme songs, poetry, symbols, quotations, and humor are powerful tools you can use to express the values and vision of your organization.

_____ Whenever possible, volunteer to stand in front of a group and speak, even if it's just to introduce someone or make an announcement.

_____ Visit your local library, or go to a store that sells CDs, tapes, and videos. Check out or buy several famous speeches by leaders who have been inspirational. Learn everything you can from the masters.

_____ Take a public speaking class. Join Toastmasters (a community-based organization that helps people become more comfortable speaking in public and expressing their ideas in a supportive atmosphere).

_____ Identify a couple of successful people on your campus or in your community who are good public speakers or who are inspirational to you. Interview these people about how they developed their communication skills. What's the source of their own inspiration?

Checklist for Challenge the Process

_____ Volunteer for a tough assignment. Be proactive in looking for chances to stretch yourself and learn something new.

_____ Make a list of every task you perform. For each of these, ask yourself, "Why am I doing this? Why am I doing it this way? Can this task be eliminated or done significantly better?"

_____ Make a list of all the things you do in your organization (or club, team, group, program, community) that fits this description: "That's the way we've always done things around here." For each of these, ask yourself, "How useful is this practice to doing our best?" If the answer is "absolutely essential," then keep it. Otherwise, find a way to change it.

_____ Hold a meeting with your teammates. Ask them what really annoys or bugs them about this organization. Commit to changing three of the most frequently mentioned items that are hindering success.

_____ Try one or two experiments (doing something that you are not currently doing). Make them small but see what you can learn from them for future experiments (and eventually new practices).

_____ Go shopping for ideas. Call your counterparts in another organization, at another school, or in another community, and find out what they are doing. Better yet, go visit them in person (and take some others with you). Find one or more things that they are doing very well that your organization could and should copy. Then follow through.

_____ Tell people what the key milestones are so that you and they can easily see progress.

_____ Use analogies. Help others at the beginning get started by visualizing what their project will be like. It's like planning a vacation: Think about how great it will be to get there and start making plans for all the little things that will be required to make this happen. Then start taking action on those little things.

_____ Identify a couple of successful people on your campus or in your community who excel at taking risks and experimenting. Interview them about what they think are the ingredients for innovation. Ask them how they get away with "breaking the rules."

_____ Spend time in an Outward Bound or similar wilderness-adventure program.

_____ Eliminate the phrase "That's the way we did it last year" from your discussions. Review annual projects and programs to improve, change, or confirm how you are proceeding.

Student Leadership Practices Inventory Facilitator's Guide

Checklist for Enable Others to Act

_____ Find ways to increase interaction among people in your organization (or club, group, unit, team, class, program, community) who need to work more effectively together. Have a potluck dinner. Teamwork and trust can be built only when people interact informally as well as formally.

_____ Establish easily accessible meeting areas that encourage people to interact. Locate the coffee pot, popcorn maker, or microwave oven between people who should talk with one another.

_____ For the next two weeks, commit to replacing the word "I" with "we." Leadership is a team effort, not an individual effort. "We" is an inclusive word that signals a commitment to teamwork and sharing. Use it liberally.

_____ Assign important tasks to others. Don't always hog the limelight. Let someone else make a key presentation. Coach and support that person.

_____ Ask for volunteers. Give people choices. You build commitment when people don't feel forced into taking action. You build motivation when people feel like they're in control.

_____ Keep your door open all the time (except when you must discuss an extremely private personnel matter). Closed doors send a signal that you don't want to interact with others, breeding distrust and suspicion.

_____ Remove unnecessary steps in any approval process.

_____ Interview an athletic coach. Ask how you might apply the coach's methods in your organization. What does it mean to "coach"?

_____ Choose someone on your campus or in your community who's known as an exceptional "people person." Accompany and observe this person for a few hours. Ask for tips on how you can do better.

_____ Take a course in team building or a class on listening skills, consulting skills, or running effective meetings.

_____ Mentor new members in your organization. Pair experienced leaders with emerging leaders.

Checklist for Encourage the Heart

_____ Wander around your "office location" for the express purpose of finding someone in the act of doing something that exemplifies the organization's standards. Find a way to recognize that person on the spot.

_____ Plan a festive celebration for each small milestone your team reaches. Don't wait until the whole project is finished to celebrate.

_____ Ask your teammates to help design a reward and recognition system for your organization (or group, club, project, community, chapter). Talk with others about how they would like to be recognized for their accomplishments or successes.

_____ Give people tools they can use to recognize one another, such as index cards or notepads printed with the message "You made my day" or "You are a hero." Create a culture in which peers recognize peers.

_____ Be creative about recognition and rewards. Try photographs, buttons, banners, ribbons, stuffed animals, painted rocks, special T-shirts, hats, and so on.

_____ Say "thank you" when you appreciate something that someone has done. Write at least three thank-you notes each week.

_____ Attend an award ceremony for someone on your campus or in your community and make notes on what you like about it. Try some of the same methods the next time you hold an award ceremony.

_____ Ask for advice and coaching from someone you know who's much better than you are at recognition, saying "thank you," and celebrating.

_____ Take an improvisational theater class. Take a class on creativity, drawing, painting, or photography to build your expressiveness skills.

_____ Ask people in your organization how and when they like to be recognized. Create a list with this information and distribute this throughout the organization.

_____ When you receive a thank-you note about someone in your group, make it public by reading it out loud at a meeting, posting it on a bulletin board (with an additional note of appreciation from you), or publishing it in your newsletter or Web page.

APPENDIX D

Comparative Data for the *Student LPI*

The following information is updated at least annually. For the latest data on various comparison groups, please go to our website, www.theleadershipchallenge.com. All of the information below refers to mean or average scores for the various sample populations, as reported in various specific published research studies.

Student LPI Scores for Greek Chapter Presidents (*N* = 177)

Model the Way	23.66
Inspire a Shared Vision	24.07
Challenge the Process	23.08
Enable Others to Act	25.58
Encourage the Heart	25.54

Student LPI Scores for Resident Assistants (*N* = 333)

Model the Way	23.25
Inspire a Shared Vision	20.66
Challenge the Process	21.74
Enable Others to Act	25.20
Encourage the Heart	22.23

Student LPI Scores for Peer Educators (N = 152)

Model the Way	23.15
Inspire a Shared Vision	23.16
Challenge the Process	22.34
Enable Others to Act	25.76
Encourage the Heart	25.36

Student LPI Scores for Student Body Presidents (N = 35)

Model the Way	23.63
Inspire a Shared Vision	24.34
Challenge the Process	23.86
Enable Others to Act	25.43
Encourage the Heart	24.57

Student LPI Scores for Orientation Advisors (N = 78)

Model the Way	23.14
Inspire a Shared Vision	24.85
Challenge the Process	23.04
Enable Others to Act	25.94
Encourage the Heart	25.49

Student LPI Scores for High School Students (N = 151)

Model the Way	22.01
Inspire a Shared Vision	21.89
Challenge the Process	21.62
Enable Others to Act	24.72
Encourage the Heart	24.18

Student *LPI* Scores by Gender

	Males (N = 378)	Females (N = 484)
Model the Way	22.30	23.48
Inspire a Shared Vision	21.18	22.52
Challenge the Process	21.65	22.63
Enable Others to Act	24.54	25.79
Encourage the Heart	22.31	24.44

Student *LPI* Scores: Reliability Data

	Internal (N = 1,255)	Test-Retest (N = 37)
Model the Way	.68	.91
Inspire a Shared Vision	.79	.93
Challenge the Process	.66	.94
Enable Others to Act	.70	.95
Encourage the Heart	.80	.96

APPENDIX E

Scoring Software Instructions

The *Student LPI* does not need to be manually or hand-scored. *The Student Leadership Practices Inventory Scoring Software* is available at an economical price (from Jossey-Bass); it is simple to use, and it makes data entry painless. The output is not only more substantial than the output for the hand-scored version, but also more aesthetically pleasing and visually easy to interpret and understand.

Following is a suggested design for using the computer-scored results in the workshop process. This design would replace the steps listed for Score and Interpret the *Student LPI* in Chapter Five. Sample output pages are included in this appendix. The output pages are also available as a PowerPoint presentation on the *Student LPI* Scoring Software CD-ROM. The software program provides a selection of up to sixteen separate pages to print out, or not, for each participant. Considerably more output is possible for each participant than is feasible with hand-scoring.

In the following text, we assume that all sixteen of the possible pages are printed out (but, again, this need not be the case). The title for each page is printed at the top of the page. Page numbers are printed on the bottom left of each page. The software automatically numbers each page in the print-out sequentially (hence participants would be unaware that any pages are "missing" if they were not selected). Note that there will only be fourteen numbered pages if all the pages are printed (the cover page and table of contents are un-numbered pages).

1. Having explained the Kouzes-Posner leadership framework and assured the students that the *Student LPI* is a valid and useful instrument, distribute to students their copies of the *Student LPI* Feedback Report. Since there is a cover sheet for each person, students can assist in handing these out without compromising anyone's confidentiality.

2. Ask students to direct their attention to you for a few minutes while you explain how to interpret the data each student has been provided. Assure the students that they will have time for further study and reflection on their feedback.

3. Ask students to look at the Five Practices Data Summary page (page 1) from their *Student LPI* Feedback Report (Sample Output Page 1). Beginning with this page, each page has the person's name ("Profile for . . ."), school or class name, and current date at the top right.

4. Direct students' attention to the first column labeled "Self." This column indicates the student's assessment of his or her own behavior on each of the five leadership practices (Model, Inspire, Challenge, Enable, and Encourage).

Explain that each of these scores can range from a low of 6 to a high of 30. This range results from calculating the lowest and highest possible total response to the six statements for each practice, using a 5-point scale where a response of "1" indicates that the behavior is rarely or seldom used and a response of "5" indicates that the behavior is very frequently or almost always used.

5. Ask students to look at their scores in this column. If you're using Sample Output Page 1 as a visual, label this column "A." Ask participants to write "1" by the highest score in this column and to continue to rank the scores in this column from 1 for the highest score to 5 for the lowest score.

Ask students to consider that the practices they ranked 1 and 2 represent the leadership practices (and accompanying behaviors) they feel *most comfortable* with or that feel most natural for them. Similarly, ask students to consider that the practices they ranked 4 and 5 represent those practices (and behaviors) that they feel least comfortable or most awkward with, that they might underappreciate the importance of, or that represent missed opportunities for participation.

Note: Step 6 through Step 8 require that students have feedback from other people (*Student LPI-Observer* scores). If only *Student LPI-Self* scores are available, these next three steps should be skipped. In any case, encourage students now to collect more data, especially from other people, if they really want to know more about their impact as leaders.

6. Ask students to look at the column labeled AVG (an abbreviation for "Average"). This column represents the average (mean) scores of all the people who completed the *Student LPI-Observer.* That is, if you added up the scores across the row marked "Model" under the "Individual Observers" columns, ("O1," "O2," "O3," "O4," and so on), then divided by the number of people who completed the *Student LPI-Observer,* you would arrive at the average (mean) score (e.g., 22 + 17 + 28 + 24 + 25 = 116/5 = 23.2). If you are using Sample Output Page 1 as a visual, mark the AVG column with the letter "B."

Ask students to look at their scores in this column. Ask them to place the number 1 by their highest score in this column and to continue to rank the scores in this column from 1 for the highest score to 5 for the lowest score. Now ask students to consider that the practices they ranked 1 and 2 represent those leadership practices (and accompanying behaviors) that *other people* feel they engage in most frequently and with which they are *most comfortable* or natural.

Ask the students to consider that the practices they ranked 4 and 5 represent those practices (and behaviors) that *other people* feel they engage in least frequently and are *least comfortable* with, or that they feel most awkward with. Or perhaps the student underappreciates the importance of that practice or has missed opportunities for participation in that area.

7. Continue by asking students to look next at the relationship between the rank order of their *Student LPI-Self* ratings and their *Student LPI-Observer* average ratings and to note the similarities between these two rank orderings. On the Sample Output Page 1 visual, you can write the letter "C" between your marks for columns "A" and "B" and ask students to think about the extent to which their self-perceptions are consistent with the perceptions of the people with whom they work and interact (as noted in the *Student LPI-Observer* scores).

Disregarding the absolute scores for a moment, this reflection focuses on the match (or mismatch) between self and others' perceptions of "reality" (leadership). You can ask students:

> Which of these two columns (A = Self or B = Observer) is the better representation of reality? If I didn't know you, but only had the *Student LPI* scores provided by you and provided by other people who interacted with you, whose scores would I consider the better representation of how you actually behave?

The response from students generally will be "the scores or assessments of others," and this is true.

That is why it is important to look at the degree of agreement between the two rank orderings. Even though there may be differences between the absolute scores from the Self and Observer columns (that is, "25" is not the same as "23.2"), it is possible that both parties will agree on the rank order of this practice, indicating agreement on the strength of this leadership behavior versus the others.

In the example provided for the group, the absolute scores do differ from one another but the rank order is identical. You will want to point this out to the group, noting that while improvement is still desirable in the various leadership practices, this sample student's own perceptions of strengths and areas for improvement are consistent with the views of others.

8. Point out the columns under Individual Observers labeled "O1," "O2," "O3," "O4," and so on. These are the actual scores on the five practices from

each person who completed the *Student LPI-Observer*. This allows students to see the overall assessment of their leadership practices by each individual *Student LPI-Observer* respondent. Students can note where there is agreement and disagreement among these respondents about their strengths and areas for improvement in these leadership practices.

This is a good point at which to explain to the students that the *Student LPI-Observer* respondents are not individually identified and that often people wish they knew exactly who these individuals were so that they could better understand the feedback. We suggest encouraging students to resist the desire to figure out the identities of particular individuals. Point out that it is more important that students attempt to understand what this person or these people are trying to tell them. In any case, earlier research indicates that participants were three times more likely to be wrong than right when trying to successfully match scores with possible Observer respondents.

Explain that the trade-off is generally between identification (nonconfidentiality) of respondents and quality of data. *Student LPI-Observer* respondents are more likely to give better (more honest, more candid) responses—positive as well as negative—when they don't have to worry about being identified. We have opted for high-quality data. At the end of this session several strategies for collecting more data and finding out more from these particular people about their opinions of one's leadership effectiveness are offered.

9. The next page of feedback, The Five Practices Bar Graphs (Sample Output Page 2), provides the summary information from the previous page (Sample Output Page 1) in a graphic rather than purely numeric fashion. Some students will get more out of these bar graphs, which easily display agreement and gaps between Self and Observer (AVG) responses, than they will from a table of numbers. Some facilitators and teachers, however, treat these pages (and there are six of them) as optional.

Note: By default the Leadership Behaviors Ranking page and the Percentile Ranking page print as the last two pages of the report unless the Ranking/Percentile at Front box is checked in the Page Select menu before printing.

10. Direct students' attention to the Leadership Behaviors Ranking page of their *Student LPI* Feedback Report (see Sample Output Page 3). On this page are the thirty leadership behaviors arranged vertically from most frequent to least frequent, according to the average responses to these statements from their observers.

Have students pay particular attention to the last ten leadership behaviors. These are the ones that hold the greatest promise for improving the student's leadership effectiveness. Students should also be aware of their top five leadership practices and should be encouraged to continue practicing these behaviors.

Call students' attention to any asterisks in the Observer column at the far right. These indicate a difference equal to or greater than 1.0 between their self-perception and the perceptions of others. Students may want to think about how to reduce the gaps between these two perspectives. Note that in some cases the Self scores will be higher than those from Observers, and, in other cases, Observer scores may be higher than Self scores.

11. Ask students to look at the Chart for Graphing Your Scores (page 21 in their workbooks) and also the Percentile Ranking page (Sample Output Page 4). The "S" in each column represents their total score for that leadership practice. A solid line connects all five "S" marks. When *Student LPI-Observer* data has been collected, then the graph will also include a dashed line connecting the "O" marks in each column. The "O" represents the average score from their observers in this leadership practice.

The Percentile Ranking provides students with a visual picture of the match between their self-perceptions and the perceptions of others about their leadership practices.

- Attention should be directed to how parallel the two lines are—indicating relative agreement about both strengths and areas for improvement.
- Attention should be directed to leadership practices for which there are significant gaps between Self and Observer ratings—indicating areas for improvement.

12. On the Percentile Ranking page, explain the percentile scale at the far left. The percentiles represent the scores nationwide from students who have completed the *Student LPI-Self*. As scores are *normally distributed* (in the classic bell-shaped curve), most people's scores fall at the fiftieth percentile (roughly half of the scores fall above and roughly half of the scores fall below), and nearly two-thirds of all scores fall within one standard deviation of the mean.

Give students a few moments to look at the data on the Percentile Ranking page and compare themselves *normatively* with other students. Although this is interesting (and often requested by students), it should be pointed out that this comparison doesn't necessarily say much about leadership for any particular person in any specific organization, organizational context, college, or university. (You may want to note the various specific student population data available in Appendix D and on the website, in the event that it is relevant to the student population you are working with).

Because leadership is a skill, you will want to point out that the important point for students is to determine what it will take for them to improve their base level of leadership ability, regardless of where they are relative to others.

Option: The *Student LPI Scoring Software* does compute average scores and standard deviations for both *Student LPI-Self* and *Student LPI-Observer* scores for *all* students in a workshop (see Sample Output Page 5). Note that this report must be printed separately and is not part of the individual student feedback reports. (See software instructions on how to print a group summary.) It is sometimes more relevant (and interesting) for students to compare themselves with their peers in the workshop. If you desire, you can distribute this information to all students, or, when asking students to examine their own scores, you can hand out or display this particular group's scores (rather than the sample group summary).

Some interpretation of the group scores should be provided. If you are going to be offering multiple leadership development workshops, you may find it useful to accumulate the data from individual sessions and develop a campus *Student LPI* profile. Some facilitators and teachers show how the particular group (or class) they are working with compares to the previous set of students (or organizational officers or campus leaders).

13. Pause for a moment and make certain that everyone is ready to continue going over the *Student LPI* Feedback Report as one group. Remind them that in just a few moments you will stop talking and give them some quiet reflection time for further understanding the impact of their leadership feedback.

14. Ask the students to turn to the Model the Way Data Summary page in their *Student LPI* Feedback Report (see Sample Output Page 6). This page reveals the six statements (leadership behaviors) that make up the Model the Way leadership practice scale. This page follows the same format as the Five Practices Data Summary page and can be interpreted in the same way. For example, on the first statement the sample person's own response was 5, while the average response from others was 4.0.

15. The next page, Model the Way Bar Graphs, presents this same data in a bar graph format (Sample Output Page 7). Some students may find this format easier to make sense of than the numerical data feedback page.

16. Have students look at the specific responses to these statements and circle any of their own and/or others that are marked with either a "1" or a "2." Suggest that these behaviors especially represent opportunities for improvement.

17. Explain that each of the subsequent leadership practices has a Data Summary and Bar Graphs page. Students should carefully work through these pages on their own, noting the leadership behaviors (statements) that they see as strengths and those they see as problematic or as areas for improving themselves as leaders.

To facilitate this individual assessment and interpretation, ask participants to look at the Exploring Specific Leadership Behaviors section in their workbooks (pages 23–24). These pages provide space for students to make sense of their feedback and to begin thinking about actions they can take to improve their leadership skills.

18. Point out that after working through their feedback on the five leadership practices they should consider again their overall leadership strengths and areas for improvement. Chapter Five in their workbooks provides space where they can write summary comments on what they see as their strengths and areas for improvement.

19. Now it's time for you (the facilitator) to stop talking. Let students know that this is their time to review their *Student LPI* Feedback Report individually, reflect on their data, and make notes to themselves in their workbooks in response to the questions asked. Provide students with sufficient time to accomplish this. This is also a time for any individual student to ask the facilitator any specific questions he or she has about the feedback received.

You now have several options on how to proceed, depending on the time available and on your learning objectives.

20. You can ask students to continue with their individual analyses through the Action-Planning Worksheet (Overhead 11) on pages 30–31 in their workbooks. Alternatively, you can convene everyone at a particular time to focus their attention on this worksheet.

21. Start by offering students some suggestions for moving from analysis to action. You may want to use Suggestions for Meeting the Leadership Challenge (Overhead 10), which is on page 29 in the workbooks. There are ten suggestions, two for each leadership practice, that we have proposed as suggestions for getting quickly started on taking leadership actions. You can say a word or two about each suggestion, providing an example or illustration.

We find it helpful to ask students to put a check mark by each idea that they think they could do *right away*. Then we suggest that students select one or two of those that they checked and complete the Action-Planning Worksheet for how they will put these suggestions into practice in their organization (or club, group, team, community, project).

Also, in Appendix C there are expanded checklists of ideas for implementing each leadership practice, which you may want to use here or elsewhere in the workshop. The checklists can also be distributed as handouts or made into overhead transparencies.

Although students can use these ideas immediately, you might instead suggest that students use these ten suggestions as a starting point for brainstorming other ideas that will make even more sense for them in their own circumstances.

22. Encourage students to select at least one leadership practice or behavior in which they can improve and to create an action plan for doing so.

Note: The Action-Planning Worksheet can be completed as a take-home assignment following the workshop or class. It can also be used as the basis for a follow-up leadership development program.

The Five Practices Summary

This page summarizes your Student LPI scores for each Practice. The Self column shows the total of your own responses to the six statements about each Practice. The AVG column shows the averages of all your Observers' ratings. The Individual Observers columns show the total of each Observer's ratings. Scores can range from 6 to 30.

	Self	AVG	01	02	03	04	05
MODEL the Way	26	23.2	22	17	28	24	25
INSPIRE a Shared Vision	21	17.6	17	13	23	16	19
CHALLENGE the Process	24	21.4	21	14	24	23	25
ENABLE Others to Act	23	20.0	22	14	21	21	22
ENCOURAGE the Heart	25	22.4	21	18	27	24	22

Observer
AVG Average of all Observer ratings

The Five Practices Bar Graphs

These bar graphs, one set for each Practice, provide a graphic representation of the numerical data recorded on The Five Practices Data Summary page. By Practice, it shows the total score for Self and the average of all Observers. Scores can range from 6 to 30.

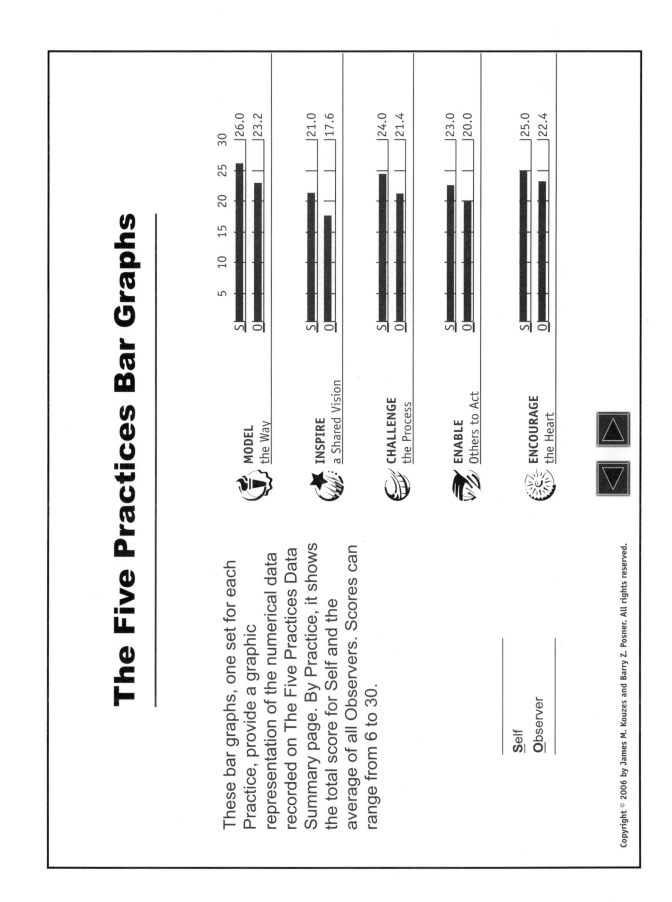

__S__elf

__O__bserver

Leadership Behaviors Ranking

This page shows the ranking, from most frequent ("high") to least frequent ("low") of all 30 leadership behaviors based on the average Observers' score. A horizontal line separates the 10 least frequent behaviors from the others. An asterisk (*) next to the Observer score indicates that the Observer score and the Self score differ by more than plus or minus 1.0.

The rating scale runs from 1 to 5
1 - Rarely or Seldom
2 - Once in a While
3 - Sometimes
4 - Often
5 - Very Frequently

	Practice	SELF	Observer
High			
3. Develops skills and abilities	Challenge	5	4.2
15. Provides support and appreciation	Encourage	5	4.2
20. Publicly recognizes alignment with values	Encourage	5	4.2
21. Builds consensus on values	Model	5	4.2
1. Sets personal example	Model	5	4.0*
4. Fosters cooperative relationships	Enable	5	4.0*
6. Aligns others with principles and standards	Model	5	4.0*
10. Encourages others	Encourage	5	4.0*
29. Provides leadership opportunities	Enable	5	3.8*
11. Follows through on promises	Model	4	3.8
16. Gets feedback about actions	Model	4	3.8
28. Takes initiative in experimenting	Challenge	4	3.8
30. Creatively recognizes people	Encourage	4	3.8
8. Helps others take risks	Challenge	5	3.6*
12. Talks about vision of future	Inspire	5	3.6*
13. Keeps current	Challenge	3	3.6
27. Communicates purpose and meaning	Inspire	5	3.4*
9. Actively listens	Enable	4	3.4
23. Sets clear goals and makes plans for projects	Challenge	4	3.4
26. Talks about values and principles	Model	3	3.4
— horizontal line —			
2. Looks ahead and communicates future	Inspire	4	3.2
19. Supports decisions others make	Enable	4	3.2
25. Celebrates accomplishments	Encourage	3	3.2
5. Praises people	Encourage	3	3.0
14. Treats others with respect	Enable	3	2.8
18. Asks "What can we learn from mistakes?"	Challenge	3	2.8
24. Provides others freedom and choice	Enable	2	2.8
17. Finds common ground	Inspire	3	2.6
7. Describes ideal capabilities	Inspire	2	2.6
22. Is an upbeat and positive communicator	Inspire	2	2.2
Low			

Percentile Ranking

This page compares your Self scores and those of your Observers to the scores of several thousand people who have taken this version of the Student LPI. The horizontal lines at the 30th and 70th percentiles divide the graph into three segments, roughly approximating a normal distribution of scores.

__S__elf
__O__bserver

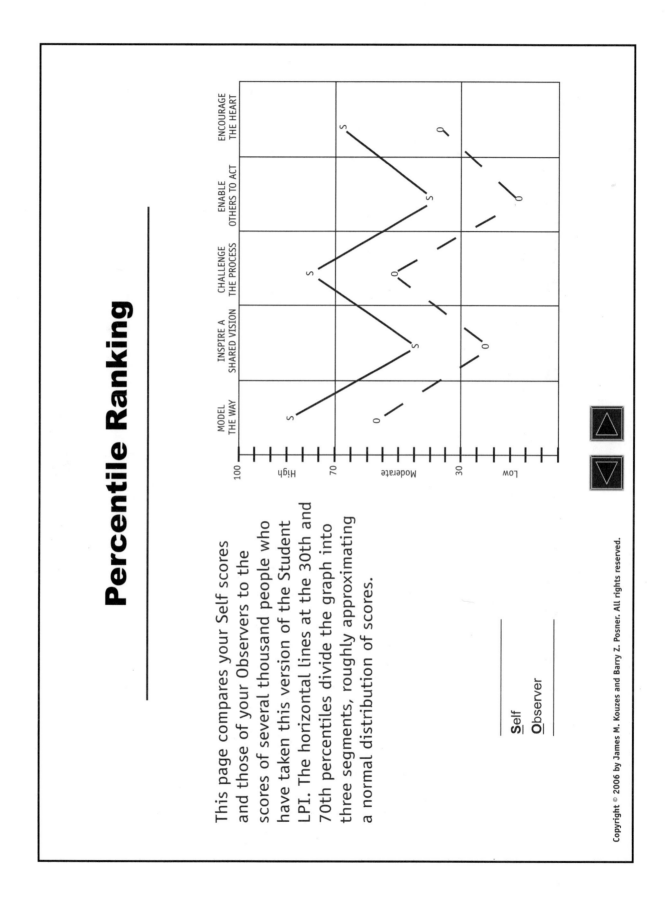

The Five Practices Group Summary

This page displays the average Self and Observer scores for all individuals participating in this workshop or other organized leadership development session. The AVG column shows the averages of all of the group's Observers' ratings for each of the Five Practices. The STD DEV indicates the extent of agreement among all individual leaders and their Observers.

Leader Surveys Tallied: 3
LPI Observer Surveys Tallied: 5

		AVG	STD DEV
MODEL the Way	S	22.7	3.1
	O	23.2	4.1
INSPIRE a Shared Vision	S	19.7	3.2
	O	17.6	3.7
CHALLENGE the Process	S	20.3	3.5
	O	21.4	4.4
ENABLE Others to Act	S	21.3	2.9
	O	20.4	3.4
ENCOURAGE the Heart	S	22.0	3.0
	O	22.4	3.4

Self **O**bserver

AVG Average of all Observer Ratings

STD DEV Standard Deviation

Copyright © 2006 by James M. Kouzes and Barry Z. Posner. All rights reserved.

ⓘ Model the Way Data Summary

- *Find your voice by clarifying your personal values*
- *Set the example by aligning actions with shared values*

This page shows the scores for each of the six leadership behaviors related to this Practice. The Self column shows the scores you gave yourself for each behavior. The AVG column shows the averages of all the Observers' ratings. The Individual Observers columns show the each Observer's rating for each behavioral item. Scores can range from 1 to 5.

	SELF	AVG	O1	O2	O3	O4	O5
			INDIVIDUAL OBSERVERS				
1. Sets personal example	5	4.0	4	3	5	4	4
6. Aligns others with principles and standards	5	4.0	4	3	5	4	4
11. Follows through on promises	4	3.8	3	2	5	4	5
16. Gets feedback about actions	4	3.8	4	3	4	4	4
21. Builds consensus on values	5	4.2	4	3	5	4	5
26. Talks about values and principles	3	3.4	3	3	4	4	3

The rating scale runs from 1 to 5
1 - Rarely or Seldom
2 - Once in a While
3 - Sometimes
4 - Often
5 - Very Frequently

Model the Way Bar Graphs

- *Find your voice by clarifying your personal values*
- *Set the example by aligning actions with shared values*

The set of bar graphs for each of the six leadership behaviors related to this Practice provides a graphic representation of you and your Observer's average ratings for that behavior. Scores can range from 1 to 5.

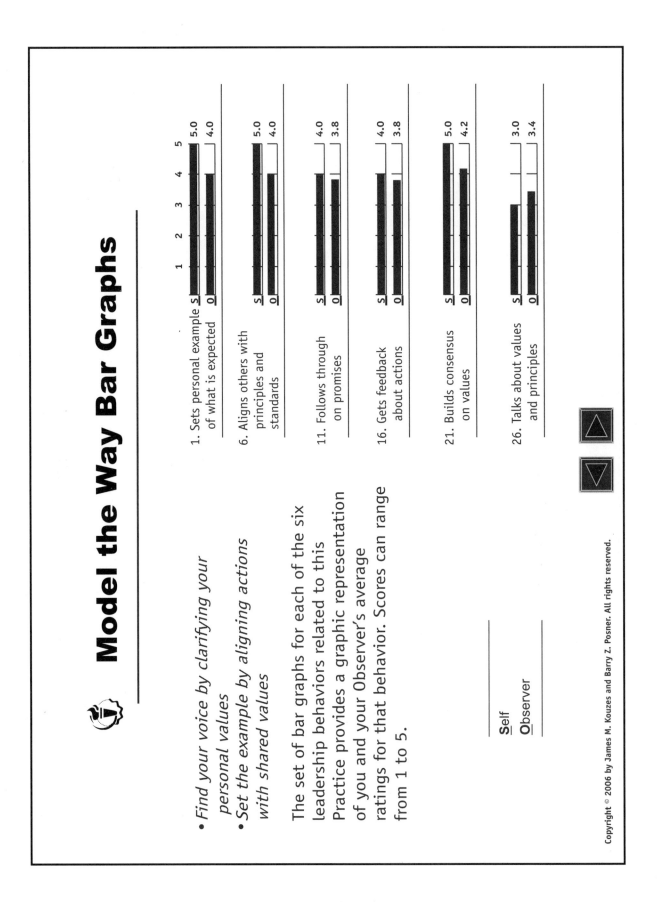

	1	2	3	4	5	
1. Sets personal example of what is expected	S					5.0
	O					4.0
6. Aligns others with principles and standards	S					5.0
	O					4.0
11. Follows through on promises	S					4.0
	O					3.8
16. Gets feedback about actions	S					4.0
	O					3.8
21. Builds consensus on values	S					5.0
	O					4.2
26. Talks about values and principles	S					3.0
	O					3.4

<u>S</u>elf
<u>O</u>bserver

About the Authors

James M. Kouzes and *Barry Z. Posner* are the authors of the award-winning and best-selling book *The Leadership Challenge.* In addition, they have coauthored a number of other books on leadership, including *Credibility: How Leaders Gain It and Lose It, Why People Demand It*—chosen by *Industry Week* as one of the year's five best management books—as well as *Encouraging the Heart* and *The Academic Administrator's Guide to Exemplary Leadership.* Jim and Barry also developed the highly acclaimed *Leadership Practices Inventory* (*LPI*), a 360-degree questionnaire assessing leadership behavior. The *LPI* is one of the most widely used leadership assessment instruments in the world. More than 300 doctoral dissertations and academic research projects have been based on The Five Practices of Exemplary Leadership® model.

Kouzes and Posner were named by the International Management Council as the 2001 recipients of the prestigious Wilbur M. McFeely Award. This honor puts them in the company of Ken Blanchard, Stephen Covey, Peter Drucker, Edward Deming, Francis Hesselbein, Lee Iacocca, Rosabeth Moss Kanter, Norman Vincent Peale, and Tom Peters, previous recipients of the award. In the book *Coaching for Leadership,* they were listed among the nation's top leadership educators. Kouzes and Posner are frequent conference speakers, and each has conducted leadership development programs for hundreds of organizations around the globe, including Alcoa, Applied Materials, AT&T, Australia Post, Bank of America, Bose, Charles Schwab, Cisco Systems, Community Leadership Association, Conference Board of Canada, Consumers Energy, Dell Computer, Deloitte & Touche, Egon Zehnder International, FedEx, Gymboree, Hewlett-Packard, IBM, JobsDB-Singapore, Johnson & Johnson, Kaiser Foundation Health Plans and Hospitals, Lawrence Livermore National Laboratory, L.L. Bean, 3M, Merck, Motorola, Network Appliance, Northrop Grumman, Roche Bioscience, Siemens, Sun Microsystems, Toyota, U.S. Postal Service, United Way, USAA, Verizon, The Walt Disney Company, and VISA.

Jim Kouzes is an Executive Fellow at the Center for Innovation and Entrepreneurship at the Leavey School of Business, Santa Clara University, California. He is also the chairman emeritus of the Tom Peters Company, a professional services firm specializing in leadership development. Jim is featured as one of the workplace experts in *What Works at Work: Lessons from the Masters* (1988) and in *Learning Journeys: Top Management Experts Share Hard-Earned Lessons on Becoming Great Mentors and Leaders*. Not only is he a highly regarded leadership scholar and an experienced executive, but he was also cited in the *Wall Street Journal* as one of the twelve most requested nonuniversity executive education providers to U.S. companies. A popular seminar and conference speaker, Jim shares his insights about the leadership practices that contribute to high performance in individuals and organizations, and he leaves his audiences inspired with practical leadership tools and tips that they can apply at work, at home, and in their communities. Jim can be reached at jim@kouzesposner.com.

Barry Posner, Ph.D., is dean of the Leavey School of Business and professor of leadership at Santa Clara University, California, where he has received numerous teaching and innovation awards, including his school's and his university's highest faculty awards. An internationally renowned scholar and educator, Barry is the author or coauthor of more than one hundred research and practitioner-focused articles in such publications as *Academy of Management Journal, Journal of Applied Psychology, Human Relations, Personnel Psychology, IEEE Transaction on Engineering Management, Journal of Business Ethics, California Management Review,* and *Business Horizons.* Barry is on the editorial review boards for the *Journal of Business Ethics* and *Leadership Review.* Having consulted with a wide variety of public- and private-sector organizations around the globe, Barry currently sits on the Board of Trustees for the San Jose Repertory Theatre and the Board of Directors for Advanced Energy (NASDAQ: AEIS). He has served previously on the Board for the American Institute of Architects (AIA), Public Allies, Big Brothers/Big Sisters of Santa Clara County, Junior Achievement of Silicon Valley and Monterey Bay, The Center for Excellence in Non-Profits, Sigma Phi Epsilon Fraternity, and several start-up companies. Barry can be reached at bposner@scu.edu.

More information about Jim Kouzes and Barry Posner and their work can be found at their website: www.theleadershipchallenge.com.